SUCCESSFUL
LOW PRESSURE
SALESMANSHIP

Edward Berman

Englewood Cliffs, N. J.
PRENTICE-HALL, INC., 1957

© COPYRIGHT, 1957, BY

PRENTICE-HALL, INC.

ENGLEWOOD CLIFFS, N.J.

LIBRARY OF CONGRESS
CATALOG CARD NUMBER: 57-7844

PRINTED IN THE UNITED STATES OF AMERICA

86305

To My Wife, GLADYS . . .

. . . from whom I learned
life's greatest lesson . . .
make haste slowly.

Acknowledgments

My humble thanks and appreciation to
FRANK B. WALKER, for his wisdom and invaluable encouragement;

GEORGE LITTLE, for his advice and low pressure philosophy;

JOE ADAMS, for his patience, suggestions, and cooperation.

They helped to make this book possible.

Preface

No moment of time is wasted; no prospective customer ever displeased; no hope for an eventual repeated sale of goods and services ever lost when friendliness, courtesy, consideration, and cooperation go to work for the successful low pressure salesman.

Leo Durocher, formerly the stormy petrel of major league baseball, once said, "Nice guys finish last." Dwight D. Eisenhower, Jack Benny, Perry Como, and many thousands of others have proven beyond a doubt that "Nice guys are more apt to finish first!" So it is with all successful low pressure salesmen, whether they are selling statesmanship, humor, music, or goods and services.

Will Rogers, the epitome of low pressure salesmanship, said, "When I die, I want engraved on my gravestone, the following epitaph: 'I joked about every prominent man of my time, but I never met a man I didn't like.'" This, I believe, sums up the entire secret of low pressure selling, for you cannot be liked by those you wish to sell, unless you apply a sincere self-desire to like, understand, and serve people.

Every book has a premise, a reason for being written. The chief premise of *Successful Low Pressure Salesmanship* is, "It pays to be nice to people." When a premise proves itself out, as it does in this book, with factual, field-tested examples, we can only say, "Here is an opportunity

v

for you to examine its logic, prove to yourself that this book will help you become a successful, admired, and respected low pressure salesman.

Successful Low Pressure Salesmanship attempts to put selling and salesmanship in a completely realistic light. It does not hold with the push, shove, and club tactics of high pressure. It does not profess to contribute a golden or magic key to overnight success. Selling, like any other profession requiring skill, study, practice and more practice, also requires constant effort, lots of hard work, planning, and a well rehearsed, dynamically presented sales story or demonstration. In this way, you can sell anything from a lollipop to a locomotive.

Low pressure selling is a career with a great purpose . . . being nice to people, getting them to like you, getting them to like buying from you, getting them to keep on buying from you. With it, you never have to judge a customer by his silence. You let him judge you by yours! With it, you are able to apply the science of listening, the art of word economy. You are able to understand what people look for in a product, a service, and a salesman. But most important of all, to make low pressure selling work for yourself, you must first be dedicated to selling, regard it as an important profession, and be ever proud that you are one of the people who help keep the economy of the entire world in balance.

Using the low pressure pluses in this book will help you to improve your low pressure salesmanship techniques. These low pressure patterns will help you earn more money and make more customer friends whether you sell a product or service; whether you sell sugar pills to hypochondriacs or dogmas to students.

E. B.

Table of Contents

vii

10. How You Can "Tell It Faster—Sell It Faster" Through Low Pressure (cont.)

1. The Secret of Successful Low Pressure Salesmanship

Low pressure selling is the quiet, courteous, and friendly science of using convincing reasons why a customer should buy a product or service from you instead of someone else. It is like a low pressure tire. It enables you and your prospect or customer to enjoy the route of the sale in complete comfort. It helps to relax the sale because it is quiet and friendly in appeal—profitable to all salesmen who use it.

I believe we'll all agree that low pressure selling is making a comeback. Radio and television commercials are getting quieter, thus indicating the trend towards low pressure in these mediums of mass selling.

There's more to prove that low pressure is becoming a fast growing therapy in these noisy, swift-moving times. The *Wall Street Journal* ran a front-page story about the boss who fired his top saleswoman.

When sales sagged sharply last fall, the owner of a woman's apparel shop in Florida came up with an unusual countermeasure: He fired his top-selling clerk. "She was my only high pressure saleswoman, and I don't believe in high pressure," he said, "Sales have increased every month since she left."

More on the front page of the *Wall Street Journal:*

Another opponent of high pressure selling is the operator

1

of a music store in Dallas. "People are relaxed when they come into my little store," he says. "This makes selling easier." The owner started in business ten years ago with $4,000 in capital, expects this year's sales to top $100,000.

Low pressure selling is the gentle art of getting the customer to sell himself. With it you can move mountains of merchandise and gain customer confidence and respect. With it you can radiate enthusiasm and gain more friends, more customers, more repeat business.

What Makes a Low Pressure Salesman?

**An honest and sincere
compliment brings low
pressure to life**

When the chairman of a benefit sends you a letter stating, "Your presence will add prestige to this benefit dinner," that's low pressure! Note how he added warmth to the invitation by complimenting you. And, even though you are expected to send your check for the enclosed tickets, the blow has been softened, the sale placed in a low pressure atmosphere.

Whether you sell or buy, using the honest and sincere compliment is the low pressure way to get along with people. For example:

"Thanks for giving me such a good hair cut."

"We enjoyed the last steak you delivered."

"That gas you sold me gave me more miles than I've ever gotten."

"The car you sold me is a honey! Rides like a charm!"

"My! You certainly do good work on my shirts!"

"That's certainly a good shoe shine!"

Giving praise where it is due is sometimes more satisfying than a larger tip to a waiter or a barber. It's a good low pressure sales habit. Whether you sell insurance, real estate, or fish hooks, the people from whom you yourself buy are also prospects for what you sell. They have their eyes on you. Make them say, "My, he's such a nice, friendly person. It's a pleasure to do business with him!"

Don't spare the compliment! That makes low pressure selling come to life.

Being complaint-considerate is a low pressure trait

When a major airline admits its error in handling my luggage, expedites the matter swiftly, and handles my claim to my complete satisfaction, they prove they are complaint-considerate, low pressure minded. The following letter is a prize example of low pressure salesmanship on their part:

> Dear Mr. Berman:
> Thank you for sending the itemized list of articles you purchased in Colorado Springs as a result of your misplaced luggage.
> Attached is our check for $43.83 in full reimbursement. Thank you for allowing us to complete this matter to your satisfaction. Given the opportunity, I am confident we can be restored to your confidence.
>
> Sincerely,
>
> Asst. to Vice President
> Transportation Services

The last sentence in the letter is the ultimate in low pressure! I am restored to their confidence. I have told many of my friends about this letter. I am now a walking, talking, good advertisement for that airline!

**How low pressure
gets appointments faster**

The bigger they are, the harder they fall. Especially when you use low pressure in writing for an appointment. For example, back in April of 1950 I sent the following low pressure letter to the publisher of a top flight fashion magazine:

> Dear Sir:
> Would you be willing to match a few moments of your busy time against hearing about a perfectly grand promotion idea.
> The writer has served an apprenticeship of almost 20 years in advertising, sales promotion, public relations, and publicity, and, because of this, feels that your ear will be pleased.
> Sincerely,

Did it work? I'll say it did! Low pressure always works! Here's the reply to my letter:

> Dear Mr. Berman:
> We would be most happy to hear your promotional idea and, if it is convenient, please do try to stop in at two o'clock on Friday. If this is not convenient, please call for another appointment. Many thanks.
> Cordially yours,

So you see, with low pressure every salesman can attract interest, attention, and result-getting action from top management all the way down the line. A quiet and informative approach to selling never fails!

**Why low pressure salesmen
earn the buyer's respect**

There is an old Latin proverb, "Caveat Emptor," meaning "Let the buyer beware!" People who buy from low pressure firms and their salesmen seldom, if ever at all, have to worry about legal technicalities if something goes wrong with the product or the service. Unfortunately, there are high pressure firms and high pressure salesmen who skip rather swiftly over the "fine print," making lots of glowing promises they never fulfill.

Back in 1950 a leading New York hospital fell prey to the dishonest wiles of a High Pressure Henry. The salesman had a "deal" for a "price." The purchasing agent was new to the job. The salesman talked fast. The buyer listened too slowly. End result—Henry got the sale. But he'll never repeat!

The hospital, operating on direct electrical current, purchased 40 freezer units, wired for alternating current only!

Did the salesman or his company make good? Did they offer to return the hospital's money or replace the units with DC motors? NO, THEY DIDN'T! Will the manufacturer of these units ever sell another hospital within telephone range of the purchasing agent? I'll let you be the judge.

Low Pressure Larry would have handled himself quite differently. He would have discussed all of the problems, the needs and requirements of the hospital. He would have sold his product on its merits. "Deals" and "price" would have no bearing on high quality, complete and uncompromising satisfaction in the sale, servicing, and guaranteed performance of the merchandise.

How planning is part of the
low pressure selling character

For example, here's how Low Pressure Larry handles a planned sales call:

"Here's how we worked out your requirements, Mr. Evans. Your market has 25,000 families. Our current national selling rate shows that we are getting around 25 per cent of the total business in this brand. We figure you might consider a potential customer total of 6,000 homes in this area. Based on these factual marketing figures, Mr. Evans, what is your opinion on ordering additional stock for the coming, busier, fall selling season?"

Need we ask what an astute merchant will do in the above case? He will sell himself. Note how Low Pressure Larry used such pleasant, pin-drop phrasing as "we figure you might consider" and "what is your opinion on ordering." Larry's last selling sentence called for the customer's opinion. He made the customer feel important. He wanted the sale to travel a two-way street. He got the customer into the act! These are low pressure selling traits that help get the prospect to sell himself.

Let us not overlook Larry's knowledge of the market, the potential. He also knows the customer's ability to stock and finance. He doesn't oversell. He states facts. He builds greater confidence because he is well armed with sound marketing and merchandising advice. He plans his call before making the contact. He's not a "hit and run" high pressure salesman!

What part product knowledge plays in low pressure

The customer asks High Pressure Henry: "How often will I have to renew the batteries in this portable radio?" "Not very often, sir," says Henry. "They're heavy duty type; they'll give you real long service." *Wrong answer!* Just small talk by a salesman who doesn't know his product, wants a fast sale, and is even willing to play havoc with facts to fool the customer.

Low Pressure Larry handles the same question: "According to factory specifications, sir, these batteries will last up to one year with average use of the instrument. Of course, you may have to replace them sooner, and it would probably pay you to have a spare set on hand just in case."

Note how Low Pressure Larry offers factory-product information. He doesn't misrepresent his product. He is step-up minded, ready to sell a spare, emergency set of batteries. He gains customer confidence by being honest and informative—all of which helps to make him a successful low pressure salesman.

How the High Pressure Salesman "Operates"

Twenty-five years of selling the low pressure way have taught me that high pressure selling is hit-and-run salesmanship. Down through the years, we have all made our own observations of High Pressure Henry and his selling sins. Here's my list: (It would be fun to make up your own.)

"Quick package" sins

1. He's a one-shot boy, a fast-buck boy. Often too aggressive, overly impudent, and rather careless with the selling truth.
2. I've never yet seen a salesman who *sold for price only,* who wasn't a high pressure salesman.
3. I've yet to see a high pressure salesman get repeat business from the customer he once pressured and sold.
4. I've yet to see a high pressure salesman make a sale who, when asked questions he *couldn't answer about his product or service,* tried fast double talk as a substitute for facts.

Bragging sins

1. He plays big shot and, boy, does he tell you how important he is!
2. He knows everyone the customer knows, only more intimately! Wait'll you hear about the "deals" he's made with friends of yours.
3. He's got connections. Lots and lots of them! Listen to the names he's dropping!
4. He has social position. Wait'll you hear the country club list he gives you.
5. He went to the best schools and plays at being a job snob by rapping his competitors for making "stupid claims." However, he treats you just like a country cousin.

Personality sins

1. He flatters you. Tells you how important you are. He thinks you're the greatest, but you should hear what he tells your competitor!
2. He's controversial. He never *discusses* the point, always wants to *argue* it.
3. He's not interested in your problems, only his own. He considers getting your order as the only problem involved in the sale.
4. He never stops *talking long enough* to recognize the sound of his customer's voice.
5. He doesn't know how to handle a *customer complaint* without almost involving his firm in a law suit. This type also includes high pressure credit managers who think *written or verbal blackjacks* are good substitutes for friendliness and understanding in their letters and telephone approaches. You know the type: "Pay up or else!" "I'm sorry, but that's your problem." "Let me tell you . . ."

6. I've yet to meet a high pressure salesman who told me he believes in high pressure selling. This proves that even a high pressure salesman hates to admit he is one!

(It'll also be fun to compare your list with mine.)

Never underestimate
your customer

Let's not kid ourselves! The smart buyer is on guard against the high pressure salesman. I know you are. I know I am. We all are. You can spot him a mile away. Especially if we've already been singed, toasted, or even burned by him.

Products and services sold the high pressure way are never sold on their respective merits. High Pressure Henry operates with a wide open smile, a wide open order book. He keeps the order book wide open so he can push you into it that much easier! He writes a faster *single* order than any salesman alive. He writes the slowest *repeat* business in selling!

High pressure selling is dangerous to the good health of any sale. It is more apt to confine the sale of a product or service to cut rate, cut price, or "deal" selling. Thus it definitely tends to undermine the meaning of product quality, extra value for higher price, and complete, customer satisfaction through better-made merchandise, dependable service, and reliable, customer warranty protection.

The ten keys that prove the low
pressure salesman's service
to the customer

1. Low Pressure Larry develops stronger sales muscles and gives them better tone by selling the merits of his product or service first. He justifies the price before quoting it.

2. I've never seen a low pressure salesman lose a sale because of price.

3. I've never seen a satisfied customer dissatisfied with price.

4. I've yet to see a low pressure salesman fail to get repeat business from customers he formerly sold the low pressure way.

5. I've yet to know a low pressure salesman who didn't have his regular customers demand by name his personal services on repeat business. Incidentally, this goes for men and women visiting their favorite barber, beauty operator, or shoe, auto, or insurance salesman, plus hundreds of other cases where the low pressure salesman is traditionally sought after because he was easy to buy from and made them enjoy spending their money with him. You can reassure yourself that this is the truth by simply examining your own reasons for spending your money with certain firms and the people in them. The thing that motivates all of us in purchasing is first, the need or desire for what we want. Second, the factor of finding people who are friendly to our buying interests. You know what we look for—a low pressure salesman!

6. I've never heard a low pressure salesman speak out of both sides of his mouth at the same time in double-talk fashion. If asked a question about his product or service to which he has no ready answer, he will be honest with the customer. He will not attempt to generalize or switch the conversation. He will tell the customer he doesn't know, but he'll try to find out. This may delay making the sale right then and there.

But it doesn't delay respect and confidence from the customer, who feels he is being treated with honesty.

7. I've never met a low pressure salesman whose tongue has grown longer from excessive usage since he became a salesman.

8. I've yet to meet a customer sold the low pressure way who was ever refused adjustment, repair, replacement, or a refund if nothing else satisfied. On the other hand, I've yet to meet a customer sold by a hit-and-run, high pressure salesman, medicine man, or carnival hawker, who ever managed to get his money back.

9. He trades up to more value for the customer's money. He describes and demonstrates product features and their benefits. He does all this first. He radiates confidence by the enthusiasm he himself shows for the benefits he wants the customer to own. Like the Amana Freezer people, he doesn't sell Amana, he translates Amana features and their benefits into "better living." He knows that people are convenience-minded. He proves that, because of the extra convenience and quality benefits in his product or service, the customer can be convinced that high quality is the best economical bargain in the world!

10. He knows how to put his sale in a friendly, relaxed atmosphere.

It is rather interesting to report that more than 50 billion dollars is earned annually by the insurance and the automobile businesses in this country and that each of these businesses, though furiously competitive, is basically founded upon low pressure salesmanship. Why? They sell their services and products on a friendly, personal-contact, repeat-business basis.

Ask yourself how many times you did, and are still doing, business with the same insurance agent. Ask yourself how many times you repeated with Ford, Chevrolet, Buick, Dodge, Oldsmobile, Chrysler, Cadillac, or Lincoln. Then, ask yourself how many times you bought from the same dealer, the same salesman. Doesn't this hold true with the family doctor, butcher, barber, clothing salesman, or shoemaker?

Why Do We Deal with These People Regularly?

It isn't too difficult to figure out. We like them because they are friendly, because we get along well with them. They respect our product and service wants. We have confidence in them. They know their job. They know how to keep us satisfied. If we complain, they handle our complaint swiftly and fairly. They never try to push us into their cash registers. They are low pressure salesmen.

What with advertising in magazines, newspapers, television and radio commercials, billboards, highway signs, and displays in windows and on counters all constantly hammering away at people, not to mention door-to-door salesmen, telephone salesmen, direct mail solicitation for products, services, and charity, it would appear that John Q. Public today is attacked and browbeaten from every side. In fact, it seems that old John Q. has found it almost impossible to dodge advertising.

A well-seasoned low pressure salesman is fully aware of the pressurized sales leverages. That is why he tempers his sales approach until it is quiet, relaxing, and pleasant to the customer. In a measure, he employs what we might call "a change of selling pace." The pace is not so swift. There is no attempt to squeeze more sales pressure into his customer's already overcrowded mind. He gives the buyer a chance to collect his wits. He helps to keep the sales atmosphere breathable and unconfining.

How patience can get you in tune
with your customer

The best example of patience I can give you on "a change of selling pace" that will certainly help a low pressure salesman become successful is the case of any salesman protecting his sale the low pressure way by saying:

"That's the story, Mr. Baker. Why not think it over? When would it be convenient for me to get your final decision?"

That's what we call a real, honest-to-goodness, low pressure "change of selling pace." Let's think about what our low pressure salesman just did! Imagine his telling the customer to think it over! Naturally, this is not a technique for over-the-counter selling. But it definitely fits high dollar spending. It's one of the secrets of successful low pressure salesmanship and *the one secret you must never forget!*

In thousands of cases involving the purchase of new homes, additional life insurance, annuities, new cars, or other high-dollar products and services, the prospect expects that you will give him some time to think about spending his money—especially large sums.

By telling the customer you would like to have him think it over, you have anticipated him. He was just about to tell you he'd like to give the matter some more thought before making a final decision. He appreciates people who anticipate his thinking, his needs. They are in tune with him. They are better able to understand his needs, his problems, and serve him accordingly. He is inclined to admire your low pressure approach to selling.

After all, if he says, "Never mind, go ahead and make up the order now," you're still way ahead.

How long has it been since you said, "Don't decide now,

think it over. I'll get in touch with you whenever you say!"

How can he fail to appreciate your low pressure change of selling pace? He will remember you for it. It will become your low pressure trademark with him. By contrast, it makes you outstanding because he's being hit from all sides by High Pressure Henry who's always geared to get the order NOW!

All of us in selling know that one quick sale, simply for the sake of getting a single order, means very little. Steady, repeat business with the same satisfied customers is profitable. It indicates a long-range, low pressure viewpoint.

As a final note in our review of the secret of low pressure selling, I contend that every sale, like every salesman, has its own central nervous system. Low pressure selling acts to lessen tension, reduce irritability and restlessness. It assures more restful selling to both the customer and the salesman. It is the most potent and profitable tonic to better selling yet discovered.

2. How the Low Pressure Salesman Uses His Product Knowledge to Build Dynamic Demonstrations

The low pressure salesman studies his product—gets to know how it is made and why it is styled the way it is. What its customer benefits are. How it can be sold successfully against competition. How he can demonstrate the benefits of the product or the service to the customer. Yes, our low pressure salesman knows not only what his own product or service offers, but also what the competition's offers. That's important because it's almost a certainty the customer may make a reference to another brand, another service, another price.

Our well-informed low pressure salesman is ready—not to quote a price—no, sir! He sells his features first through DYNAMIC DEMONSTRATIONS! He makes his product or service literally "jump through the hoop" for a customer. He talks product, its customer benefits. He demonstrates the product features and gets the customer into a possessive frame of mind. Now he's ready to quote the price.

If he didn't care to study, if his first and last concern was price—maybe even a "deal" at cut price—if he doesn't care to be patient, care to trade up to value and quality for lack of time and bother involved, he's strictly a one-shot boy. He's just not a salesman, because he's violating all the rules of best selling. He's talking into his own ears and is rather pleased with this distorted, one-way conversation. He's also heading for the place all bad salesmen go—DEAD END!

Why Product Knowledge Is a Must

Because the product or service represents the tangible elements that will be exchanged for customer dollars, the salesman must know everything there is to know about his product or his service.

Enthusiasm, confidence, integrity, demonstration and all the other sale-making characteristics of the salesmen and their company surround the sale, but have no dollar-value measurement, either in the customer's pocketbook or in the annual financial statement of the firm. To be realistic about it, we must know our product as intimately as we know ourselves. Without this knowledge, we ride and sell from an empty wagon. Here are some points to illustrate how product knowledge clinches a good low pressure sale:

1. You, the alert, well-informed low pressure salesman would never permit your product or yourself to be taken for granted by the customer.

2. Place the sale in a quality atmosphere by proving that the quality of your product is worth more because it offers more. Then you prove your statements by demonstrating the visible value differences.

3. You sell the product as being better than others because it has more quality benefits, more features, more conveniences that save time and operating dollars.

4. You sell all the extra quality and convenience benefits before discussing price. This keeps your sale on the quality track.

In connection with extra benefits, I would defy the greatest salesman in the world to sell a Cadillac to a customer if the car had no cigarette lighter.

How to play "worth more because" to the hilt

Selling most products that cost more usually fits in with the "worth more because" approach. The product is made of wood instead of plastic. Because the food space is larger —the motor larger. Because the cooling maximum is greater. Because the car has power steering and power brakes. Because the leather is finer, the last more durable. Because the bristles won't fall out as fast, you will get a softer, more comfortable shave. Because the cabinet or piano or dresser is a hardwood mahogany veneer, not pine, plastic, or masonite.

At this moment, I should like to offer a couplet to you. It represents something I have discovered in low pressure selling. Here it is:

> Remember your customer's head isn't hollow;
> Examine its thoughts—a sale will follow.

This is another way of saying find out *first* what your customer wants to hear, then start selling.

I believe this is an excellent low pressure rule-of-thumb. So many of us take our customers for granted. Many salesmen fool themselves by thinking the customer is out for the salesman's scalp and the thing to do is scalp the customer first! A good salesman knows that customers must be pleased, but he will not sacrifice his product or his salesmanship by permitting price to become the primary factor in the sale. He has also discovered through valuable experience that customers will buy properly if they are sold properly.

This brings us to something that has been bothering me

for a long time. I'm sure all of us know that we get less when we pay less. That could apply to salesmen as well as customers. If price, which seems to be the fetish of all high pressure salesmen, were the most important part of sale making, all of us, salesmen and customers, would be riding around on motorcycles. All of us would be wearing identical suits, hats, and shoes. Everyone would be living in three- or four-room bungalows, cooled only by electric fans, heated by coal or kerosene stoves. We would all consult our dollar watches for the time and still be listening to radio with cats' whiskers, crystal detectors. Things would be monotonous indeed!

Primarily, and this goes back as far as time itself, people buy extra benefits, extra conveniences, extra pleasures. In many cases, they even duplicate their purchases. For example: two cars, two air conditioners (perhaps three or four). Homes, clothing, insurance, jewelry, books, radios, television sets, phonograph records, and hundreds of other items, for in-home or in-travel usage prove that people desire their conveniences and pleasures in multiples.

How to Focus a Sale: Know Your Product—Show Your Product!

Up to now, we have asserted that a "price" salesman doesn't know his product as well as he should, that he doesn't sell his product primarily upon its own merits, and that he seldom shows his product or service to the customer in the most favorable selling focus. For example, when the customer walks in and says: "I'd like to buy a briar pipe."

"This one's a terrific buy! Just reduced from $5.98 to $2.98," he replies. He points to a group of briars on the counter. He never lets up! Keeps right on talking. "Yes, sir, friend, this is the kind of pipe that will make your friends sit up and take

notice! Terrific deal! You oughta buy a couple of
'em. They're really swell!"

This is a typical example of selling out of focus. Imagine
yourself as being the underestimated, ear-beaten customer.
You didn't get a word in edge or otherwise. All you wanted
was a briar pipe. Suddenly, everything changed. You
found yourself in the midst of a federal case. You wanted
a briar pipe. You were in the mood to buy. You weren't
looking for a cut-rate price or deal. You only wanted a
good, substantial briar pipe!

No wonder that this salesman can't understand why his
briars never seem to move. Even at reduced prices! He
would be a lot better off if he stopped yapping long enough
to listen! He might hear the customer say: "Can't you
show me something better?" Especially customers who've
indicated a positive willingness to buy for desire, convenience, and pleasure instead of price.

Suppose we set the same scene for a product-wise, low
pressure expert and see how he handles a sale like this one:

"I'd like to buy a briar pipe."

"We have a complete selection, sir. May I show
you several of our latest imported models?"

"Sure, go ahead. Mine's due for a change.
That's why I'm here."

"Here's one that's made of the oldest and finest
briar. It's hand finished in the natural grain."

"Mine doesn't have a filter. How about this
one?"

"Oh, yes. It's a detachable type filter. Let me
show you how it works."

The salesman proceeds to remove the filter. He also
shows the customer how the newer type of screw assembly
fits more snugly. He gets his customer into the act, too.

"How do you like the weight of this one?" he asks, as he hands the pipe to the customer.

"Seems a bit too heavy," replies the customer.

"How's about this one in the same styling?"

"Yes, that's a lot better. I'll take it."

Don't be surprised if Larry sells this customer a pipe rack and humidor, a pipe pouch that matches, and even a suede pipe glove. Why? Well, there are several low pressure reasons. Larry knows his product. He shows his product. He takes an interest in pleasing the customer. You might say our pipe example doesn't hold with automobiles, insurance, or many other higher priced items. The truth is, no matter what you sell or when you sell it, making the customer feel you are interested in his needs does more to eliminate the price barrier than anything else!

I don't think we have to dwell too long on the respective sales techniques of these two salesmen. You saw what happened. One knew his product and used his knowledge to best advantage. He sold from the top down (the pipe he displayed and demonstrated was priced at $10). He didn't rely on cut price. He realized that the average pipe-smoker, like a dog fancier or stamp collector, takes a special interest in the pipes he buys because pipe-smoking is like a hobby, and, therefore, a pipe-smoker wants to know more about the product than a cigarette or cigar smoker.

Note that he didn't monopolize the conversation. He let the customer say something and get the feel of the product to see if the weight of the pipe was satisfactory. He relaxed the sale by being friendly to his customer's needs. He sold from the top price by describing the quality features of his merchandise. He also sells related items, a cardinal rule in step-down or step-up merchandising.

I've used the pipe sale as my very first, product-knowledge example because at the end of 1955, a wire service story appeared in the nation's newspapers concerning the pipe business. An executive in this industry stated, "56 million dollars in extra pipe sales and related pipe items were lost at the retail level because of poor salesmanship."

How to Get the Customer
to Participate in the Sale

Whether it is pipes or shoes, tires or tractors, rayon or rubber, knowing your product and showing it at its best quality advantages enhances the buying desire of the customer. This is part of the low pressure idea of making your product and service features seem so very important that the customer, in turn, feels you regard him as an important person since he merits such thorough, courteous, and saleable low pressure treatment.

Getting the customer into the act is another way of saying the sale is the stage; the product or service, the actors; the customers, the audience. Like a good showman, you've got to make the customer feel that he belongs to the play, that he is more than a part of the audience. You've got to make him part of the story—one of the leading players.

If you're selling pianos, let the prospect play. We know you're pretty good at the keyboard, but, after all, don't ham up the sale! The fastest way to sell a piano is to let the prospect get into the act of playing it. Then, he becomes the star. Be a good audience. In most cases, people coming to purchase a piano are quick to sell themselves before they get to the piano store. Pity the salesman who likes to give a "little" concert while the prospect stands to the side, becoming disgusted and impatient. Goodbye sale if the concert wears thin.

The piano sales technique applies to erector sets, vacuum cleaners, radios, high fidelity and television sets, record players, washing machines, electric razors. For that matter, it applies to any product sold where the prospect may participate in holding or handling or operating the controls of the item. Of course, if you discover he is not familiar with the operation, you brief him before you let him do it. That's how you get him into the act!

Some salesmen use this pet phrase, "It costs only a few pennies more to go first class." However, it's always harder to just say something and expect people to be impressed by what you say. It's always easier to prove what you say through the drama of demonstration, through *customer participation*. In other words:

Getting the customer into the act makes him sell himself

Getting the customer into the act during the sale is a surefire method of clinching the sale. It is a vital part of the low pressure approach to selling. Why? Because, in this manner, the customer is bound to sell himself sooner. This also gives the low pressure salesman a better opportunity to prove that his product is worth more before he mentions that it costs more. Let's not kid ourselves! We know that higher priced hats and shoes and suits fit better because they are made to fit better, last and wear longer. With the customer in the act, he feels the fit, the cut, the drape, the last, or the softness of the material—has a first-hand look at the workmanship. It gives the sale a "prove-it-to-yourself" atmosphere.

Let's take a look at how our low pressure clothing salesman gets his customer into the act.

You've decided to buy a suit. In this case, a ready-to-wear garment. You enter the store. The salesman greets you cordially, introduces himself, gets to know your name. He asks you to step over to the first rack of clothing.

"I'd like to try this jacket just to get your size."

The coat fits beautifully! You're wondering how he managed to guess your size so well. Don't underestimate him! Remember, he's had plenty of customers with a build like yours.

"How much is this suit?" you ask.

He inspects the price label, hesitates momentarily.

"This is a hand-tailored imported cashmere. It is the latest in 3-button styling, and we have it in gray, brown, or ebony. This suit sells for $125."

You're a bit pale for a second. Perhaps there's a slight lump in your throat. But you manage to gulp down the lump and say, "I'm sorry but I didn't expect to spend so much."

Don't worry about it. The salesman's on your side! He gently reassures you that he only wanted to get your suit size, remember?

Somehow, while all this is happening, the fit of the coat feels better and better. Lots of room in the back and shoulders. Plenty of sleeve space. The drape of the coat is excellent. The material soft to the touch. Slyly, you've peeped into the mirror and you see what you want to see. A smartly fashioned Beau Brummel! Boy! You feel and look wonderful! In fact, you feel just as important as the president of General Electric.

Still gracious and friendly, Low Pressure Larry moves you away from the higher priced suits.

"Let's try this one for size," he says. How you hate to remove that first jacket!

Now, you try on the second coat. It pinches a bit in the shoulders. Not too much, but it's noticeable. This one doesn't drape as well as the other. The material isn't as soft. The sleeves seem a bit tighter. We know this isn't hand tailored. Hand stitching has vanished. It isn't imported.

"How much is this one?"

"$98.50," says Larry. "Of course, it isn't hand tailored or

hand stitched, but it does have most of the features of more expensive clothing." He tells you about the weight of the cloth, the convertible pockets, the choice of colors.

"Still too high for my budget," you tell him.

"That's perfectly all right," he says. "Let's go over here and try on another number."

You now try on a suit that costs $69.95. When he helps you on with it, you begin to understand why you need some help. The shoulders, sleeves, front, and back are as snug as a strait jacket! You've had your chance to compare three different suits. Need we ask which of the three you'll finally select? In most cases, when the pocketbook can stand a little extra beating, you're going to pick the suit that had the best fit, the best value. The average buyer, and Larry knows this, will choose the middle price. Very few, if any, will settle for the "tight" fit when they can buy what they like better for a little more.

This is how Low Pressure Larry gets his customer into the act. He doesn't have to force his selling. He doesn't have to get into dickering or bargaining about quality. He lets the customer settle the issue himself on the basis of value instead of price. Larry uses another excellent low pressure technique. He sells from the top! Step-down selling is always easier than step-up selling. Especially when you have gotten the customer into the act.

How the Low Pressure Real Estate Salesman Gets the Customer into the Act

Real estate is sold the low pressure way by good salesmen only because our house hunters have already bumped into this treatment:

"You shouldn't pass up this wonderful deal!"

"This location is simply terrific!"

"The view from here is colossal!"

"By the time you move in, streets, sidewalks, and highways will all be completed!"

"There will be a giant shopping center only walking distance away!"

You still haven't met the first agent who was able to convince you he had exactly what you wanted. You still haven't met the low pressure salesman. That is, until today. You met him today by appointment. He had been recommended by neighbors who'd recently purchased a home through him. You had phoned him last night, told him exactly what it was you were looking for, and how much you could afford to spend. He promised to meet you today at your home. He came on time. Friendly, honest, quiet. He listened while you described additional details. He arranged a tour of several sample homes. He accompanied you.

What was the biggest reason that decided you on buying the new home from him? Low pressure salesmanship, you say? Why?

He told you to take your time about making such an important investment. He described the construction of each home you saw thoroughly and honestly. He reviewed the "fine print" in the contract so there would be no misunderstanding. But the real clincher was when he said, "As you know, most agents ask for a rather sizeable down payment in order to hold the home. I'd rather you gave me a small down payment of fifty dollars, which would be returnable, until you finally decided whether or not to buy."

I have seen this type of real estate salesman in action—especially the type of man who does such a thorough low pressure job that he is willing to stake better salesmanship against the idea of selling his properties on a higher, down-payment basis, in spite of the fact that all his competitors are asking for higher down payments.

How Dynamic Demonstrations Emphasize
Product Knowledge

The safety glass fronts of most television receivers are either tempered or laminated like automobile window and windshield glass. To tell the customer only that the glass is constructed to withstand up to two hundred pounds of impact per square inch proves that our salesman knows his product but doesn't know how to demonstrate its benefits.

Here's one way a television salesman does it. He is showing one of the higher priced receivers to a customer. Suddenly, he clenches his fist and lands a mighty blow on the glass front. Again and again, he wallops it, but the performers on the screen go right on performing without so much as a shake or a shiver.

That's selling with a dynamic demonstration! No need for a lot of talk about the strength of the glass or the solidity of the set. There's no doubt about it—one *Dynamic Demonstration* of a product feature is worth at least ten thousand words.

During the past four years, DuMont dealers, using this dramatic, customer-convincing demonstration, sold over 100 million dollars' worth of television sets. It is interesting to note that any one of DuMont's competitors, using the same type of safety glass, could have had a similar dynamic demonstration. Out of more than fifty manufacturers, I doubt if more than two or three applied this creative, value-selling approach at the retail level. So you see, even in competitive selling the difference between one product and another may sometimes be a creative, suggestive difference where the sale is made by the firm or person taking advantage of the *Dynamic Demonstration*. Even diamonds won't sparkle in a dark cellar!

The low pressure salesman realizes the sales importance of making the product jump through the hoop for his customers. He knows how to make his product come to life with *Dynamic Demonstrations*. He knows the customer is always on the lookout for extra features, extra conveniences, extra quality. This is even true of customers who go "bargain-hunting"! The real trick is making the customer feel that quality is a better bargain!

How to cross the line to more effective sales: Know how to help your customer

A good low pressure salesman must also have the courage and self-confidence to make decisions for himself and the customer. Having first evaluated the customer's needs, he must have the wisdom to act quickly toward fulfilling them.

The courage of our convictions and the extra enthusiasm to put our decisions into action make the difference between thinking of getting the order and actually getting it.

A fine line separates the salesman from his customer; the customer's money from the cash register; success from failure. The more we think about the thinness of the line, the more rapidly we realize how high pressure selling broadens the line, just as low pressure selling can eliminate the line completely.

The low pressure salesman eliminates most of the sales barriers quietly through friendship, customer confidence, and respect.

Here's an example of what bad salesmanship does to broaden the barrier to the order while making a cold turkey call—a recent experience right in my own home. It was evening, about 8 o'clock. The doorbell rang. I opened the door.

"Yes?"

"Did you get your sample copy of the *Post*?"

"No, we haven't. What's it all about?"

"We're trying to set up a route in the neighborhood."

"Well, I always buy the magazine at the newsstand, but . . ."

"I guess you don't want it."

"I didn't say that."

"Well, guess I'd better go."

"Yes, I guess you better had."

Boy did he flop! Speaking of broadening the barrier, he made it bigger than the Grand Canyon! Take a look at what he didn't do to get on the sales track:

He wasn't friendly, didn't extend a simple "Good evening, sir, how are you?"

He cut me off in the middle of a sentence when I was about to invite him inside to give him an order for home delivery of the magazine.

He remained an absolute stranger from the beginning because he didn't tell me his name.

He couldn't have cared too much about his product since he referred to it as the *Post* instead of by its full name, the *Saturday Evening Post.*

He had no patience with me, so I would be expected to show little or no patience with him.

He showed no ambition or enthusiasm because his opening remark was spoken in dull monotone.

He had no imagination because he said nothing about topical features that might be coming out in the next issue of the publication.

He invaded the privacy of my home by ringing the bell and then took for granted that he should have audience simply because I opened the door.

He acted like a solicitor instead of a salesman. I could have forgiven anything, except that!

How to make your product
jump through the hoop

I think you'll agree that the higher the price of the product, the harder it becomes to sell. For example—automobiles, insurance, tractors, and washing machines are harder to sell than chewing gum and popcorn. Items like soap, notions, canned foods, which are purchased on a demand or habit-buying basis, do not have to be made to "jump through the hoop" for customers at the point of sale. It's a different story when you get into the high-dollar class of item or service. This is the time you must be able to apply the technique of *Dynamic Demonstration!*

For example, your customer is far more interested in what your product will do for him or give him than he is in its technical construction. With a *Dynamic Demonstration,* you can melt the toughest sales resistance. This is the quickest way of proving that you have implicit faith and confidence in what your product can do when you put it to a dramatic and convincing test before the customer.

It makes no difference what you sell. More products and services can be sold more rapidly and convincingly when the customer is given a chance to sell himself first. This is the low pressure way. Just think of how many more Polaroid Land Cameras could be sold by permitting the prospective customer to operate them. Think of how many more washing machines and electric ranges might be sold through "live" washing and cooking demonstrations with the customer "in the act"; how many more automatic pop-up toasters could be sold by dealers using "live" toasting demonstrations and serving the toast with tea or coffee right then and there!

Such items as radios, high-fidelity sound equipment, record players, and television sets can be sold more rapidly the low pressure way by getting customers into the act, selling themselves long before you yourself sell them. Here's how a television salesman gets his customer to establish a preference, participate in the sale, and sell herself.

The salesman has asked the customer several leading questions to establish her preference for picture size, styling, and finish. Now he's ready to get the customer into the act:

"Now, Madam," says the salesman, "please tell me when to stop tuning in the picture for the brightness and contrast you would enjoy best at home." Saying this, the salesman begins to increase the brightness and the contrast until the customer (now participating) says, "Stop there! That's about the way I would like to see it at home."

Naturally, here is where the salesman tells his customer, "Here, madam, see how easy it is to tune this receiver yourself. You do it."

As you can see, this is a clear cut case for the low pressure salesman who knows how to handle the customer and how to make his product *jump through the hoop*. He got the customer into the act. He got the customer to sell herself on "what she would like to see at home." This is the moment for closing. He did more. He let the customer familiarize herself with the tuning controls. This will save the firm unnecessary out-of-pocket expenses for "nuisance" service calls. This is low pressure selling because you've given your product an opportunity to do some talking for you.

Main Points to Remember About How the Low Pressure Salesman Uses Product Knowledge to Build Dynamic Demonstrations

The low pressure salesman never quotes a price until he has gotten the customer into a possessive frame of mind. He knows how to make his product "jump through the hoop" for a customer. He talks benefits and then demonstrates the product features.

Why product knowledge is a must

Without product knowledge, we ride and sell from an empty wagon. Remember:

1. Product knowledge puts your sale in a quality atmosphere.

2. It helps to sell your product on its merits.

3. It helps you prove that your product is worth more because it has extra quality benefits and features that can be demonstrated.

How to focus a sale:
know your product—
show your product

Remember the story of the pipe salesman. You can sell your product the same way—from the top of the line. Remember:

1. There are customers who like to pay more because they know that when they do they get more. Your job is to tell them, with facts and with demonstrations, why the better item is worth more.

How to get the customer
to participate in the sale

Getting the customer into the act makes him a part of your sales story—gets him to sell himself faster. Remember:

1. A good piano salesman lets the customer give the concert.

2. It is always easier to prove your demonstration when the customer is doing it himself.

Remember how the clothing salesman got his customer to sell himself by using the low pressure technique.

How the low pressure real estate salesman got the customer into the act

You can sell better against competition when you review the "fine print" in the contract and give the customer time to make an important decision. Remember:

1. Product knowledge combined with a low pressure approach need not depend on a high down payment.

How dynamic demonstrations emphasize product knowledge

One dynamic demonstration of a product feature is worth at least 10,000 words. The real trick is to find out *what* demonstration of your product is the most dynamic and then be sure to use it during every selling opportunity. Remember:

1. A dynamic demonstration makes your product come to life.

2. Even customers who go bargain-hunting can be made to feel that quality is the best bargain in the world when this quality is demonstrated.

3. Even in competitive selling the difference between one product and another is often enhanced by the salesman who takes advantage of the dynamic demonstration.

3. How to Use Enthusiasm in Low Pressure Selling

The successful low pressure salesman knows that each selling word must be born in the heart, changed to a smile in the brain, made to ring like a bell in the voice. He knows how to make each product feature and customer benefit strike home like a bowling ball. Being inherently enthusiastic, he is a self-starter. He is energetic. *He goes out of his way* to do more things than are expected of him in his job. It is this extra effort, drive, and energy that make him more outstanding and well liked by the people who seek him out, for they have discovered that he is friendly to their wants and interests.

The common conception of enthusiasm

Up to now the general idea of enthusiasm in selling has been bandied about and buffeted like a small craft in a monsoon. Pure enthusiasm, found regularly in low pressure selling, doesn't mean that a salesman must literally jump up and down and clap his hands with glee to impress the customer. Enthusiasm can also be quiet, and it is more effective when it is sincere.

Back in the late twenties, a French doctor by the name of Emile Coué had the whole world repeating these words: "Every day in every way, I'm getting better and better."

33

For a long time millions of people repeated this catch phrase as prescribed, three times upon arising and three more times upon retiring at night. As you can see, this philosophy has not been sanctified by time. It fell short of the mark because it offered a panacea for improvement, but didn't stress such vital improvement makers as *hard work, knowledge, experience,* and *confidence.* For these are the qualities that produce pure, low pressure enthusiasm.

Without working hard, you cannot gain knowledge. Without the application of your knowledge, you may never be given an opportunity in high-dollar selling to gain experience. Without the experience, it is unlikely you will be able to gain confidence in yourself. With confidence, you will have developed an enthusiasm as sincere as that which prompts a man to cover his heart with his hat when the flag goes by.

How Low Pressure Enthusiasm Works Better for You

Successful low pressure salesmen will tell you, as they've told me, that they like their jobs and their work and are so enthusiastic about selling, they go out of their way many times to do little extra things for the customer. This gets them the repeat business that makes selling profitable and pleasant for everyone. For example:

- A courtesy note after the call, thanking the prospect for his time, interest, and cooperation.
- A note, in longhand, thanking the customer for the order.
- A phone call, if local, asking the customer you sold if the car or washing machine or television set or piano or typewriter is operating satisfactorily.

- A 2-cent postcard to let the customer know the approximate time repairs will be completed, when the product will be delivered, or the service begun.

- A congratulatory letter or telegram to your prospect or customer regarding his promotion in the company.

I could list many more little things and agree that you, yourself, have already thought of perhaps ten or twenty. The important thing is that every single one of them is a potential sale maker and repeat-business getter.

Why Enthusiasm Calls for "Shirt Sleeve" Thinking

There are big things you can do in high-dollar selling if you are enthusiastic enough to do them first and worry about why you did them afterward. Sounds like double talk, doesn't it? Really, it isn't.

You know as well as I that there are thousands of people who say, "That's not my job." "Why should I do it?" "I wasn't hired to do that." "Let John do it, that's his job." These are the people who won't go out of their way to please the customer. They prefer to stay in a narrow, clogged, order-taking channel that never reaches open water.

One of the big things I did several years ago helped my firm keep a friendly business association with a distributor who purchased almost a million dollars' worth of television receivers annually for three straight years.

A carload of merchandise, delivered on the day I was visiting the head of the distributorship, remained unloaded at the siding, since it had arrived when shipping and receiving employees were at lunch. A hurried call from a nearby dealer who wanted a truckload of receivers seemed to pose a problem because the last truck was scheduled to leave the warehouse for pickups before the loaders would return.

The distributor and I removed our "business" coats, then headed for the freight car. We unloaded 26 units and sent the truck on its way to the customer with his merchandise. To this day, the distributor is still telling everyone within ear-range about the man from the factory who went out of his way, and temporarily out of his job, to lend a helping hand.

This is enthusiasm at work for the customer.

How Enthusiasm Generates Sales Power

Practically everyone has a latent spark of enthusiasm within him, just as we all have a spark of every quality that makes for success. But the spark of enthusiasm needs some energizing force to bring it into action.

A child may rebel for years at practicing a musical instrument, but if he happens to have a capable teacher, he may eventually become just as interested and enthusiastic about music as his teacher. This example proves that enthusiasm can be instilled in others, providing we distill it within ourselves.

Edison was considered a dunce as a schoolboy, but a toy chemical set ignited his spark of enthusiasm and changed him from an unenthusiastic student to the inventive genius of the age.

True enthusiasm may be compared with the spark plug of an automobile. Someone has to turn on the ignition to make the spark ignite the gasoline in the engine. Without the spark, the car simply will not run. It's as simple as that. You can generate more and more sales power, personal sales profit, and sales success by making up your mind to turn on the ignition yourself. An enthusiastic salesman is like a beacon light to a buyer who just wants someone to brighten the path to the sale.

True enthusiasm, the kind that starts from the heart, sets up a chain reaction strong enough to move literal mountains of merchandise. Like all other valuable secrets of sales success, enthusiasm is not a single-action or single-calibre kind of sales ammunition. Having observed various types and degrees of enthusiasm at work, all of us will agree that there is always a time, a place, and a sales situation that calls for a certain, specific application that correctly fits the need.

In the case of Knute Rockne, it was his knowledge and pure love of football that inspired all his players to greater effort. Whether they won or lost, it can be said that they never lost a game for lack of enthusiasm. Just as it can be said that his players certainly won more than their share because of the heights of enthusiasm to which they were inspired by this great man.

A low pressure salesman selling a product or service that has a reputation and a good background of prestige and customer satisfaction doesn't have to create an earthquake to get a customer to buy.

Enthusiasm in a broad sense has been thought of as a means by which one person may impress another person to like what he is doing. If it is mechanically applied or taught on a follow-the-leader basis, the entire conception of enthusiasm is lost then and there, because in essence enthusiasm represents all the things, the sincere and pleasant things, that you can do to make the customer much happier about doing business with you.

There is such a thing as *self-enthusiasm*, enthusiasm for the product and enthusiasm for the job the salesman is doing. This self-enthusiasm is valuable both to the salesman and the customer, especially if it spurs the customer to tell others "it was a pleasure to do business with him because he likes his job so very much."

Getting the Appointment Through Low Pressure Enthusiasm

Here is an example of how a good salesman stimulates enthusiasm, interest, and curiosity when phoning his prospect for an appointment.

"Good morning, Mr. Jones. How are you today?"

"I'm just fine. Who is this?"

"My name is John Adams. I'm with the XYZ Company. We've just completed four field tests in other cities of a promotion that is selling its head off. It seems made to order for your company and I can offer you an exclusive. Could I conveniently show you this plan at two this afternoon?"

Will Jones be interested? Will he be curious? Will he give Adams an appointment? If someone called you for an appointment, using the same technique, what would you say? Remember, the salesman offered to outline a program that was making record sales in four other cities. He offered Jones an exclusive. Jones can't very well refuse to hear the story.

"How Much Do You Know About Our Business?"

You have just been asked this question by the buyer. He isn't trying to trip you. He simply wants to know if you are enthusiastic enough before your call to find out something about his business. If you came prepared, you were then ready to answer this question. Here are two examples of how enthusiasm combined with planning and preparation made a hot sale out of a cold-turkey call.

My first story deals with a salesmanager who got himself a $25,000 a year job with a British firm doing business in America because he was enthusiastic enough to go out of his way to prepare himself for the question: *"How much do you know about our business?"*

Knowing that he was to meet with the principals of the company in London, my enthusiastic friend had conducted at his own expense a quick, but nevertheless comprehensive survey of 15 dealers handling the British firm's products. Through the survey, he secured dealer reactions from questions on merchandising, packaging, and the like.

When he was being interviewed, up popped the question: "How much do you know about our business?" He was ready with the answer. The preliminary work he had done with the dealers had given him much more than a conversational approach to some of the problems faced by the company. For example, he was able to give them the answer to one of their more serious problems when he said: "Your dealers have told me they are unhappy with your present advertising campaign in the States. They don't quite understand why you stopped featuring the items which were so successful with them last year." Then he produced his survey to support his story.

Yes, he got the job. He got the job because he was enthusiastic enough to conduct a one-man survey to get it. This is the kind of enthusiasm that pays off.

The second example, dealing with going out of the way to uncover things that will help you make the cold-turkey sale, is the story of another friend who, in less than one year, has risen from sales training director to general sales manager of a large appliance firm in the Midwest. He sold himself by finding out everything he could about the problems of the firm, the industry, its distributors, dealers, and retail customers. Then at his own expense he prepared an elaborate sales presentation covering each facet of the business and demonstrating how he proposed to challenge the various problems of the company. Needless to say, the firm, which was undergoing reorganization, gave him an opportunity to make his presentation. He sold the program. He sold himself. Why? Wouldn't it be reasonable to conclude that his preparation had been spurred by an enthusiastic desire to succeed?

Why pass up the extra benefits that are sparked by enthusiasm?

There is no magic potion sold over the counter that will create and energize enthusiasm. There is no temporary tonic that can be consumed to make a salesman sincere, patient, and courteous. You manufacture your own low, medium, or high degree of enthusiasm. You do it through adding extra interest in your work, extra effort in your selling day, extra hours in your selling time. You do it by going out of your way to please friends, prospects, and customers. You keep in shape by using the same technique at home with your family. Real enthusiasm is the eternal sales spark that ignites extra sales, extra commissions, and extra dollars in the bank account, plus extra friends around you. Who among you would ignore such benefits?

How Three Billion Dollars Worth of Sales Are Thrown Away by Lack of Enthusiasm

You've no doubt read many articles mentioning that more than three billion dollars in extra sales are lost annually at retail because of unenthusiastic sales people. Here's a typical example of how extra business can be obtained when the salesman combines enthusiasm with ingenuity in dealing with captive customers.

Before we proceed, let's define the captive customer:

> If you're getting a haircut, you are a captive customer until the barber tells you he's finished cutting your hair.

> If you've asked for a jar of jelly, you are a captive

customer until the grocer places the item in a bag and hands it to you.

If you stop for gas and oil, you're a captive customer until the attendant has completed his service, taken your money, and made change.

How to use suggestive salesmanship to build customer enthusiasm

Drug stores, beauty parlors, shoe stores—in fact, any establishment with a cash register—are all in control of the customer until they've made change for the sale. This means that related items, hundreds of them in some cases, depend chiefly upon display and customer eye-attention for movement. Enthusiastic salesmen can do much to help move many of these items more rapidly through suggestive salesmanship.

Let's examine some of this suggestive salesmanship in action:

An enthusiastic and creative rust-preventive polish salesman, calling on gasoline service stations, has this technique:

He first shows the attendant what to do and what to say by actually waiting upon a customer who has stopped for gas and oil and is *waiting for his change!*

"By the way, sir, have you noticed how the chrome on your front and rear bumpers is beginning to rust?"

The customer seems quite surprised. Gets out of his car to take a look. "By gosh! You're right! They are rusting, aren't they?"

The salesman now has a clear field. "Well, sir, I've got something here that will not only remove the rust you now have, but prevent rust from bothering you again. It costs only 50 cents."

"Hmm, 50 cents, is that all? Better give me two bottles. The wife's car probably has the same trouble."

There's no deep, dark secret involved here. An enthusiastic salesman, willing to pump gas, clean the windshield for the customer, and show the attendant how to take his product off the counter and move it, displays constructive and creative low pressure salesmanship.

Just think of how many more thousands of dollars' worth of merchandise could be moved more frequently if more sales people dealing with the captive customer took advantage of their own imagination, and creative ability.

Why enthusiasm makes a low pressure salesman successful

Being fortified with selling's greatest asset—enthusiasm —the low pressure salesman pays much more attention to all the little things in making a sale. He leaves nothing to the customer's imagination. He takes nothing for granted. Every small detail has long since become an intrinsic part of his selling anatomy. He uses little things, as we use our thumbs, for selling-leverage power. Small as your thumbs are, try to tie your shoe laces without them! Try buttoning your shirt or shaking hands without using them.

Why enthusiasm comes from little things

What are these little things in selling that make up the true and profitable pattern of enthusiasm? Well, I believe that we get the best sales leverage from the human smile. One that reflects its pleasing quality in the eyes and the voice, in the over-all disposition of its wearer. Believe it or not, once you lose your smile, you lose the sale.

Naturally, there's much more to selling than smiling. But

again, and I don't think the point can be emphasized too strongly, a smile is friendly. It's quiet. Low pressure selling stands out by virtue of its quietness. A friendly, smiling salesman is welcome relief to noise-stormed buyers of today. There's always a time and a place in selling for a smile.

To repeat, start your sale with a smile. Not a grin, mind you, but a quiet lip smile. After all, with a grin on your face, the customer may think you're making fun of him. I've seen some salesmen get into trouble that way.

Remember too, you can't lip smile very well with your mouth open talking. Try to do it. You'll see a silly grin where a smile should be.

A Simple Trick to Make Yourself Easier to Buy From

Like thousands of low pressure salesmen, I too enjoy being known by my customers and friends as "the man behind the smile." Let a smile be your sales insurance. You'll find that a smile before, during, and after the sale keeps your customer in a pleasant frame of mind that is more receptive to your sales story. It also makes you easier to buy from.

Being easier to buy from is a real low pressure sale-making habit. Especially if you can make your prospect or customer feel as relaxed as he does in his bedroom slippers. Remember that Mr. Purchasing Agent or Mr. Customer may have left home that morning after the toast was burned or, perhaps, little junior cleaned daddy's favorite pipe with soap and water. Your smile may rub off. Cheer him up! At any rate, if you aren't wearing a smile when you call, you may have something to cry about when you leave; namely, not getting the order. There's another great danger when your smile is missing. The customer may feel that you aren't too happy with your own product or service. So, by all means, get behind your smile and *stay* there!

How Being Yourself First Gives
You Solid Sales Appeal

Many salesmen make the honest mistake of trying to mimic some of the actor-type, fast-buck boys who conduct courses in selling. It just can't be done. Selling is not acting. Particularly today when a salesman must specialize in the fundamentals of marketing and merchandising. Let's get the record straight, gentlemen. Lots of people are under the impression that all you have to do to be a salesman is join a country club, play a good game of golf, dress well, and live it up. This is a far cry from the truth! Selling today is the pulse beat of the economy, a hard-working and well-respected profession, one that calls for consistent, creative ability.

If you want to mimic someone else, you should try for Broadway or Hollywood—not selling. You must be yourself first, last, and always! Then go on from there to practice, rehearse, and improve your own sales knowledge and personality.

One man's food in selling can so easily be another's poison. When you try to copy another man's personality in selling, you lose your own, infinitely better personality. The result is artificial and stilted.

You'll run into the same trouble with "canned" speeches because they are better suited to the person who concocted them. So, be yourself first. Be honest, courteous, and enthusiastic with your customers. Practice your sales approach, timing, and stage presence. Always remember to *rehearse it* or *regret it*.

The much-beloved Will Rogers epitomized low pressure enthusiasm. He was a great humorist because he never pretended to be anyone else but himself. Steer clear of meaningless sales platitudes. Your own homemade phrases are more believable. Play it safe! Be yourself when you sell and, for that matter, at all other times.

How enthusiasm can be generated
in the wrong direction

Frank Walker, President of MGM Records, tells this story of enthusiasm with a reverse twist. When Frank was with another record firm, one of his field salesmen had been sending in the most enthusiastic reports about prospective business ever received by the company. As Frank put it, "They were literary masterpieces!"

As time went by, sales figures in the territory slumped. The home office was worried. The sales manager decided to check up. He visited dealers who'd been mentioned in the reports. Found out they hadn't been contacted for weeks. He visited the salesman at his home where he found him in the garage. What was the salesman doing? Jacking up the rear wheels of his car so he could let the motor run a few hundred miles on the speedometer while he either went to the movies or relaxed at home. That's carrying enthusiasm too far! Just imagine how far this same salesman could have gone if he had used his ingenuity and enthusiasm in the right way.

How a pleasant frame of mind
brings back pleasant customers

Let's be honest. If you are selling or seriously thinking of making selling your profession, don't stay in it or get into it if you can't retain a pleasant frame of mind.

You and I know that the classic statement, "the customer is always right," represents a heritage of vision for all salesmen for all times. We also know that sometimes customers can be wrong. The true low pressure salesman knows that by keeping a pleasant frame of mind, he is able to avoid this high pressure pitfall involving an irate customer. For example:

"I distinctly remember your telling me that I could return these curtains if they didn't match the bedroom color."

"I'm sorry, madam, but you're mistaken! I told you that the curtains were marked down for special sale and not returnable."

"Well, you'll just have to take them back because they don't match."

"I'm sorry, madam, you'll have to take the matter up with my superior."

So the customer leaves. Perhaps for good. Did High Pressure Henry face the customer with a pleasant frame of mind? Did he have the right answers? Hardly. Here was a case where Henry should have agreed to satisfy the customer. Instead, he used a quick brush-off technique that helped his store lose the customer and perhaps many of her friends.

Next time you're stopped for some traffic violation, for example, use a pleasant frame of mind. Your choice of escaping with no more than a lecture will be enhanced. The ticket's on its way when you tell the officer "He must be mistaken." You might even silently smile your way out of trouble. It's a fact. As soon as you argue or alibi, the officer starts writing the ticket.

Yes, although customers can be wrong and often are, the low pressure salesman relies upon his pleasant frame of mind to keep his customers satisfied. He will never argue the point or belabor it because he knows that his nearest competitor is usually the winner of any argument between customer and salesman.

Like ham and eggs, enthusiasm and a pleasant frame of mind cling together profitably. One is virtually impossible without the other. A pleasant frame of mind—it's a good formula to remember. Use it face-to-face, when you phone, or even when you are writing to a prospect.

How to get smoother "smileage" in your sales travel

Throw a pebble into a lake and suddenly the small ripples that result become larger and larger. The pattern is one of radiation. Register an enthusiastic and friendly smile in low pressure selling and it spreads just like the ripples in the lake. It becomes profitably contagious! Especially if your prospect or customer catches a smile infection from you.

This is the key to the door of all selling success! Why? Using that smile regularly throughout the sale makes the toughest buyer think you're in complete agreement with every word he utters!

Speak softly and carry a big order book

Otto Schultz, a leading salesman for the Morley Brothers Company in Michigan, one of America's largest consumer product distributors, has been selling major appliances for over 30 years. Every time Otto calls on one of his many dealer customers, he takes out his order book and places it in a convenient, eye-catching location so the dealer will be sure to see it.

Throughout the quiet, low pressure conversation that follows, there rests the order book in full view. A silent, yet very potent sales weapon which is never once referred to by Otto until he is ready to leave.

This top-secret method of silent, low pressure selling has worked wonders for Otto for 30 years, and I recommend it to you. It's a golden silence formula. A sure-fire way to tune in the customer to your order book.

Silent selling—try it today! Let your order book do some of the speaking for you. A word of caution! Don't get too enthusiastic and fill in the customer's name and address in the order book until he gives you the order. That's high pressure and it may kill your sale before it begins.

How Low Pressure Radiates Enthusiasm and Gains Customer Confidence

When you use simple, effective, low pressure selling methods in your approach to a customer, you are radiating the enthusiasm of yourself, your firm, and its services. You gain customer confidence faster because you reflect your own pleasure in what you are doing and your own liking for your company and what it sells. Because of your enthusiasm, you and your sales story both become believable. The order follows.

The successful low pressure salesman inspires customer confidence in his approach by making the sales story believable because he, himself believes it. In this way he, also, builds a firmer foundation for repeat business. Here are a few believable types of sales approaches:

- The shoe salesman who tells you that a better grade shoe at the same price will be in later in the week.
- The local grocer who says: "Please don't take those rolls. They're not as fresh as you usually like them."
- "The vanilla ice cream is too soft. I wouldn't recommend it."
- "The porterhouse has too much fat. How about this choice fat-free cut of sirloin?"
- "I'll do your hair the way you want it, sir,

but may I suggest a bit of an improvement here on the back?"

- The insurance man who says: "I wouldn't recommend the plan you selected, sir, because here is a policy that will give you three times as many benefits for just a few more dollars a year."

- The automobile salesman who tells you that it will cost you less to finance your car insurance through your bank than at the automobile dealer.

- "We guarantee our cleaning work, but I'm afraid we would ruin those gloves if we handled them."

- The rug salesman who advises against the selection you are making because it will clash with the room colors you mention.

Honesty is a part of pure enthusiasm

I believe we could put all these examples into the selling category of honesty. I am sure you will go along with me that it is pretty hard to be enthusiastic about something that is dishonest, except for confidence men, swindlers, and the like. Therefore, it goes without saying that an enthusiastic salesman is bound to radiate confidence, especially if he is an honest, low pressure salesman.

How to low pressure your way to sales popularity

Selling champions use low pressure to gain the respect, admiration, and friendship of their prospects and competitors both.

I mention competitors because they can do you more good than harm. Many successful salesmen have found that by being friendly to competitors, they are able to gain new business—customers the competitive salesman couldn't handle but sent their way because of price, service availability, or other reasons.

In spite of the false plusses given by many sales managers to their so-called "personality" hot shots, I've met more successful salesmen who lasted longer by being low, rather than high pressure popular. Give me the low pressure boy all the time. Give me the man who smiles his way into a sale, and I'll give you a man who makes twice as much money in selling. That hail-fellow-well-met stuff went out with Rattlesnake Roger—the cure-all character. The only reason the young men of today still think of salesmen as drummers is that Hollywood and Broadway are still using the same scripts they bought 50 years ago.

The medicine pitchman and the fast-buck peddler of yesterday are as strange in professional high-dollar selling today as spats or high button shoes.

Main Points to Remember About How to Use Enthusiasm in Low Pressure Selling

Low pressure enthusiasm is the inherent quality that makes a salesman want to do much more than he is ordinarily expected to do both by his employer and by his customer in making a sale. Remember:

1. Pure enthusiasm is the result of hard work, knowledge, experience, and confidence.

2. When you go out of your way to please the customer, he will go out of his way to make sure you get his repeat business.

How low pressure enthusiasm
works better for you

The little things you do for the customer are responsible for the big volume you get when you are selling. Remember these simple little things:

1. Following up your call with a courtesy note.
2. Phoning to check on customer satisfaction.
3. A note in advance to let the customer know when repairs will be completed.
4. A congratulatory letter to the prospect or customer on his promotion in the company.

Why enthusiasm calls for
shirt sleeve thinking

There are big things you can do in high-dollar selling if you are enthusiastic enough. Remember the story of how the distributor received the salesman's help in unloading a box car of merchandise.

How enthusiasm generates
sales power

Customers like the man who likes his job and who shows enthusiasm for his product and his company. Remember:

1. *Self-enthusiasm* spurs the customer to tell others: "It was a pleasure to do business with him because he liked his job so very much."

Getting the appointment through
low pressure enthusiasm

No sale was ever made until an appointment was secured to start the sale's ball rolling. Remember:

1. You can get appointments faster when you have more than just merchandise and services to sell.
2. Buyers want ideas. They want to know what others are doing with your product.
3. They want the results of the field tests and other successful programs.
4. With enthusiasm working for you, you will go to extra trouble to furnish prospects with this kind of information. Remember how John Adams did it in the telephone example.

"How much do you know about our business?"

Don't let this question hit you like a ton of bricks so that you fall beneath the masonry. Remember:

1. When the prospect asks this question, he really hopes you do know his business well enough to serve it.
2. Don't just sell *your* customers. Help them sell *theirs.* That's creative selling induced by enthusiasm and the will to prove you know how to merchandise yourself as well as your product.

How three billion dollars worth of sales are thrown away by lack of enthusiasm

The least you can do while you control the first sale is try to make the second. Remember how the rust polish salesman used this technique and even pumped gasoline to prove his sales point. Don't be afraid to roll up your sleeves to prove how enthusiastic you really are.

A simple trick to make yourself easier to buy from

A smile before, during and after the sale keeps your customer in a pleasant frame of mind, more receptive to your sales story. It also makes you easier to buy from. Remember:

1. By all means, get behind your smile and *stay* there.

How being yourself first gives you solid sales appeal

One man's food in selling can so easily be another's poison. When you try to copy another man's personality in selling, you lose your own that is infinitely better. Remember:

1. Be yourself first. Be honest, courteous, reasonable, and enthusiastic with your customers.
2. Forget "canned speeches" because they are better suited to the person who concocted them.
3. Practice your sales approach and your timing.
4. Always remember to *rehearse it* or *regret it.*

Why low pressure radiates enthusiasm and gains customer confidence

The successful low pressure salesman inspires customer confidence in his approach by making the sales story believable, because he, himself, believes it. Remember:

1. Honest enthusiasm generates customer confidence.

4. Building Customer Confidence Through Low Pressure

Customer confidence in selling is the customer trust and friendship plus the repeat business you earn by *proving* you are as anxious to *please* people as you are to sell them.

Customer confidence is no different from the confidence people entrust in each other in their social relationships. It is the same as the confidence held by patient for doctor, student for teacher, or friend for friend. Without question, customer confidence is a successful salesman's most important asset.

Customer confidence cannot be gained with gimmicks, half-facts, "bait" discounts, gifts, entertainment, premiums, or empty promises. It is not buyable, only "earnable." You must earn it by being sincere and trustworthy. You must earn it by gaining customer respect for your dependability and sales knowledge. Once you've earned customer confidence, you must preserve and maintain it. Earning customer confidence, like selling itself, is continuous—a full-time job within a job.

The fact holds true, that once you've instilled confidence in the customer's mind, your product or service is no longer a target for "price" competition. After all, who ever questions the cost of a Cadillac, a Tiffany diamond, a Stetson hat, a Florsheim shoe or a visit to a medical specialist? Customer confidence places you, your firm, its goods and services above competition from one end of the marketing line to the other.

When your product, service, or personal friendship has been customer tested and has won customer confidence, the results are repeat business and long range sales success.

How to Build Customer Confidence
by Being Dependable

If you were to ask a group of your own friends to tell you what single attribute they admired most in a salesman, I believe they would say, "dependability." They would say it because it is the same attribute that holds our society together. It represents the trust others place in what we say and do while selling, as well as the faith and trust we ourselves place in the hands of others with whom we come in contact during our daily lives. How many times have you heard people say:

- I never feel pain when he drills—he's dependable.
- His meats are always fresh. His cuts excellent —he's dependable.
- I recommend him. Been buying my cars from him for years—he's dependable.
- Cuts my hair the way I like it, and his haircuts last longer—he's dependable.
- Here's his phone number. He painted my house last year—he's dependable.
- You'll find her materials, patterns, and styles fetching—she's dependable.

Dependability is the master builder of customer confidence. It is the power generator of customer confidence. It is respected by all, admired by all. Being dependable is a full-time job. It calls for a long-range, selling viewpoint. It is a sale-making force because it produces respect and admiration for your sales honesty. It attracts the friends of the friends you've already made, so it is both a friend-maker and a sale-maker.

Dependable low pressure salesmen become successful by *pleasing* customers before they sell them, by *relaxing* customers while they are selling them, and by *keeping friendship and confidence* intact with customers after they have sold them.

You can use this simple, uncomplicated formula every day, and it doesn't cost a single penny. Especially since you obtain its basic ingredients at no cost from both the brain and the heart.

By using it regularly on all prospects and customers, you can solve the simple secret of repeat business. What is the secret? Simply this: *Please a stranger, make a friend. Make a friend, make a regular customer.* Isn't it true that all friends were once strangers? And isn't it also true that friends are less difficult to sell than strangers?

How Considerateness Breeds Confidence

Nothing is more relaxing to people than *considerateness.* Present-day tension has tripled the manufacture of sleeping pills, quadrupled nerve tonic sales. In view of this, could you think of a better, non-medical, low pressure application for relaxing customers than considerateness? Wouldn't you agree that it is much easier to sell a relaxed customer than a tense customer? Of course you would.

Like every other valuable, low pressure, sale-making quality, considerateness helps the customer to make up his mind more quickly, to sell himself faster. In a low pressure salesman, considerateness becomes his badge of recognition. It identifies him for the future, as well as the present. So it is, too, with products, services, hotels, restaurants, railroads, airlines. Here are just a few examples to prove the point:

Tourists, transient businessmen, and permanent residents enjoy and tell their friends about how each Statler Hotel has a television set in every room, a popular novel at the bedside, a lending library for their convenience, and delivery of the morning paper. These are the *rememberable* symbols of Statler *considerateness*. They breed confidence because they breed pleasure, convenience, relaxation.

People visiting the main office of the Fruehauf Trailer Company at Detroit are given a booklet by the receptionist. The first page of this booklet says, "We're pleased to have you call on us and, whether you've come to buy from us, sell to us, or just say hello, we'll try to make your visit pleasant and send you on your way happy." The rest of the booklet is written in the same, pleasant, relaxing vein, and goes on to describe what Fruehauf makes, how the company operates, sells and buys. This is Fruehauf's way of putting the customer or the salesman at ease. It is *considerateness* in action through clever public relations.

United Airlines Executive flight from Chicago relaxes its passengers by providing bedroom slippers. What could be more relaxing? The flight is smooth, the food excellent, the service superb. But we all *remember* the bedroom slippers. This is *considerateness* at work through relaxation.

Schraft's, Stouffer's, and Harvey System Restaurants breed confidence with *considerateness* when they at least wait until you've finished your cereal or grapefruit before bringing your eggs and bacon. This way, you don't wind up by eating cold eggs. In other words, they don't give you that hurry, hurry, high pressure treatment. They are considerate of your convenience. They relax you into returning as a regular customer.

Being considerate, and being remembered for it, is a low pressure, long-range quality. Short-range proprietors and salesmen may get by for a while, but sooner or later the man with a short-range viewpoint in sales and service goes into long-range retirement.

How Self-Confidence Creates Customer Confidence

Self-confidence is the reward of practical experience and constant practice. It not only creates customer confidence, but produces champions in every field of endeavor; thus we could identify self-confidence as the secret of all success.

When self-confidence is modestly projected, it radiates a feeling of ease, assurance, and security in the customer's mind. It makes the customer think—

- I'm glad to be dealing with him. He knows what he's talking about.

- My investments will be safe. His facts are sound, and he has experience. He knows what he's talking about.

- I respect his judgment because he respects my point of view. He knows what he's talking about.

- I'll buy the annuity from him. He explained it in complete detail. First time I ever understood the real value of an annuity. He knows what he's talking about.

- Glad I'm dealing with him. He'll do the best valve job I've ever had on the motor. He explained something mechanical so even I could understand it. He knows what he's talking about.

He knows what he's talking about. That's exactly what the customer thinks when he is dealing with a self-confident salesman. Actually, this is what the customer *wants to think* when he buys, because indirectly, he is also praising *his own* buying judgment. Therefore, you can relax a customer more easily through self-confidence by *knowing* what you are talking about.

How to achieve self-confidence in low pressure selling

Is there a simple, easy, and work-free way to become a self-confident salesman? Unfortunately, no, there isn't. Self-confidence doesn't come easy. Like all other success makers, it is the reward of self-willingness to gain knowledge, to secure practical experience, and to practice constantly.

Self-confidence is like a protective shield that guards all high-dollar salesmen against apprehension, uncertainty, and fear. It sets them apart from mediocrity in selling, as it does with a self-confident champion who sleeps like an infant a few hours before a championship bout.

Self-confidence denotes the absence of fear, just as fear denotes the absence of self-confidence. When you know your product or service as intimately as you know yourself, you can speak about it with self-confidence.

When you know your market, your competition, and your prospects and their buying habits, you begin to reinforce your selling knowledge with greater self-confidence.

When you keep up with industry and consumer trends, know the most modern sales techniques, and keep abreast of merchandising, sales promotion, packaging and display methods, you can pass this knowledge along to others with self-confidence.

Self-confidence doesn't come easy. But once you've

earned it, it never leaves you. No major-league ball player would dare face a ball coming to the plate at 85 to 90 miles per hour without it. No public speaker would dare face an audience of two or three hundred without it. No driver in the Indianapolis 500 would dare begin the race without it, just as no high-dollar sale can be made without it.

How to develop self-confidence through "apple polishing"

Mother Nature does an artistic job with an apple. But the wise fruit merchant isn't altogether satisfied with nature's artistry. He polishes the apples, even waxes them sometimes to make them look more appealing, saleable, appetizing.

Though the merchant's sense of beauty is confined strictly to a greater appreciation for the tinkling sound of silver as it drops into his cash register, who can deny he is truly a sales artist?

The merchant knows that by arranging his apples in neatly polished rows, they will attract attention and create a desire to buy. He knows how to make his display reflect cleanliness and variety. He knows how to create an apple appetite. He needn't shout his wares. The beauty of his display speaks for him. It is neat, shiny, silent. But it speaks just the same.

Low pressure salesmen, like our merchant, must polish their own selling apples. We could call their apples the fruits of self-confidence. By polishing these fruits—the apple of sales knowledge, the apple of experience and hard work, and the apple of practice—we are then able to inspire the confidence and the good will of all of the people with whom we come in contact to sell. Now—today—is the time to become an "apple polisher."

How to build self-confidence
through sales knowledge
and practice

If you want to join the ranks of high-dollar salesmen, you've got to work as hard at building self-confidence as high-dollar salesmen do. You must keep pace with an ever-changing selling process. True, the philosophy of selling remains basic. But it is never static, never becomes stagnant. High-dollar sales methods vary with the moods of marketing. The character of retail markets changes with the advent of new homes, new people, new merchants, and new merchandising techniques. The character of industrial markets changes with the innovation of new production methods and new methods of purchasing and selling.

To be a high-dollar salesman and arm yourself with the sale-making quality of self-confidence, you must be willing to spend the extra time and effort to obtain new sales knowledge and new marketing techniques. You must keep pace with the merchandising parade.

Self-confidence through sales knowledge makes you a sales specialist. A brain surgeon never stops studying medicine, a great concert pianist never stops practicing, a great boxing champion never stops training; they keep themselves in self-confident physical and mental trim. In other words, self-confidence is limitless and depends mainly upon how much effort you put into acquiring it and how much practice you apply in using it.

Once you have high-dollar sales knowledge, you have a tangible substance with which to practice. Self-confidence without it is as ineffectual as trying to play the piano well without knowing how to read music, or trying to sell a valuable piece of property by generalizing, or trying to pilot a ship through reef-infested waters without the knowledge of navigation.

To practice gaining self-confidence, you must first examine your selling strengths and weaknesses with the objective of bolstering the strengths and destroying the weaknesses. Once you have done this, you are ready to set up a master plan of personal navigation for self-confidence.

How to Set Up a Navigation Plan for Building Self-Confidence

1. Attend meetings at your local Sales Executives Club[1] or Sales Managers Club. These organizations are the mirrors of present-day sales knowledge. They will keep you currently informed on new, modern, up-to-date sales techniques and marketing and merchandising methods, including many other sales know-how producers of self-confidence in planned, scientific selling.

2. Participate in the public-speaking seminars held at your local sales club, Rotary, Lions, Kiwanis, Chamber of Commerce, or Evening University.

3. Attend local sales seminars and clinics sponsored by retail or wholesale trade association groups in your industry. The sales information you obtain at such gatherings gives you a cross section of valuable viewpoints and a better understanding of industry problems.

4. Subscribe to the key trade papers in your industry. Have them mailed to your home. Study them regularly. Evaluate the many good suggestions made in them. Then pass these good suggestions along to many of your customers who are always too busy to read the trade papers themselves. This builds their confidence in you.

---

[1] See Appendix for listings of sales executives' clubs throughout the U.S.A.

5. Read more and more good books on selling written by such outstanding business book authors as Charles Roth, Harry Simmons, William Damroth, Leslie T. Giblin. Read their sound, practical, and success-making methods. Then put them into practice as part of your self-confidence navigation pattern. Look into the points made by James T. Mangan in his book *How to Win Self-Confidence for Selling*.[2]

6. Try out your sales story on someone at home. Present your talk to a close friend. Ask *him* to make suggestions for improvement. Ask him to tell you what he remembered. How it appealed to him. In this way, you'll be certain to season your approach and sales talk accordingly. Make it believable, rememberable, convincing. This helps you *practice* your way into self-confidence.

7. Become more active in local civic groups such as the Parent-Teachers Association, Community Center, YMCA, YMHA, Little League, Police Athletic League. Here you meet people, exchange views, build self-leadership, as well as self-confidence; build friendship contacts that lead to perfect customer relations.

8. Plan for self-advancement through self-confidence by studying, working, and practicing harder. After all, holding a selling job, big or little, doesn't eliminate the possibility of aiming for sales management.

The field is wide open. There is as great a need for sales managers today as there is for salesmen. The opportunity for advancement in selling is as good or better than that of

---

[2] James T. Mangan, *How to Win Self-Confidence for Selling* (Englewood Cliffs, N.J.: Prentice-Hall, Inc., 1957).

any profession in America. Better, in fact, today, because this is the age of salesmanship.

How to Gain Confidence Through Customer Respect

Gaining respect to win customer confidence is another low pressure selling quality. Such special qualities as personal integrity, loyalty to firm and product, a sense of fair play, responsibility, honor, each belong in the mold that shapes the successful destiny of a high-dollar salesman. But one particular virtue stands higher than all the others in low pressure selling—the ability to capture and use the wisdom of others, including customers.

Either you stop talking long enough to capture the wisdom of someone else or you babble your way into disrespect. Certainly no high-dollar salesman ever commits this sales crime. If you want to gain the customer's respect, you must first listen to his point of view, his questions. Otherwise you must prepare to face a completely pointless situation.

The "gift of gab" is a sales misnomer. It is not a gift. The real gift is knowing when to turn on the gab and when to turn it off. You can never win the respect of a customer, or for that matter, anyone else with a steady yakity, yak yak (this is one of the greatest fallacies of "canned" sales talks), because it leaves no room for customer questions or conversation. In other words, how in heaven's name can you know what the customer wants or what he is thinking, until you give him a chance to speak up and tell you?

Another disrespectful selling sin to be avoided at all cost is overselling. You can never get the customer to sell himself by overselling yourself. When you oversell, you leave no room for the customer to relax, understand, or be in sympathy with your message. Overselling creates suspicion, makes people think "there must be a catch to it somewhere."

It is as simple as saying you and I would run into tough sales resistance if we were to try to sell 20-dollar bills on some busy, street corner for 10 dollars. Of course, people would accept them if we handed them out. But could we really *sell* them?

The high-dollar, low pressure salesman knows it isn't necessary to oversell. He lets the customer do most of the talking. He lets his product or his service speak for itself with facts.

When you let the customer tell you *what he thinks, what he knows, what he wants,* you are letting him sell himself.

The more you talk about *what you think, what you know, how good your product is, how good your firm is,* you create a mental suspicion. So the customer thinks, "It just can't be that good if he's trying so hard to sell it." Good products and services, like good low pressure salesmen, sell themselves without any overselling, pressure, exaggeration and overstatement. Good low pressure salesmen respect the knowledge, opinion, and judgment of their customers—and thus win customer respect.

How overstatement destroys confidence

I don't wish to become contentious, for that is not a low pressure blessing. But in all fairness to myself, and to you, I should like to discuss something that has been bothering me for quite some time. It is the subject of overstatement.

Advertisers and salesmen who thrive upon overstatement surely must lack confidence in themselves and their products. For some strange, mysterious reason they seem to fear that the customer must be constantly impressed and overwhelmed by sheer force of adjectives and glowing descriptions, lest he change to another product or service in 24 hours.

Is the hoopla of overstatement really necessary? Are

people impressed or convinced by glowing phrases, sug- ared descriptions in newspapers, magazines, radio, tele- vision, personal contact selling? I don't think so. If any- thing, sugar-coating your sales talk builds suspicion faster than confidence.

How understatement
inspires confidence

In the heart of downtown Chicago, there are several thousand restaurants. Many of them serve a great variety of delicious food, their prices are reasonable, and the serv- ice you get is courteous, prompt, satisfying. To a stranger in town, finding a good restaurant always seems to be a problem. Perhaps you have it, too, especially if you don't want to eat in the hotel or accept the recommendation of a cab driver who might suggest a distant location. Now I don't know about you, but I'm a reader of window menus. I like to shop them when I'm in a strange city. That's how this story began.

While reading a menu in the window, I noticed a small, neatly hand printed sign which said, *"We Have a Good Lunch Today."* A true masterpiece of low pressure under- statement!

Although I may not be the best customer guinea pig in the world, because I'm more than partial to low pressure, these six quiet, sincere words inspired the following reac- tion in my mind:

- They attracted my attention and my interest because the words were unusual in a restau- rant window. Most restaurants are content to take for granted that a sign saying "Restau- rant" is sufficient—it isn't, not if you want to stimulate interest.

- The simple modesty of the statement stimulated my confidence in the management. Made me think the food must be substantial.
- The words made me think the atmosphere inside was unhurried, free of clatter, unassuming, relaxing.
- They decided me in a fleeting moment that this was the restaurant where I would have my lunch.

As you can see, I remembered *"We Have A Good Lunch Today,"* just as I will always remember *where* I saw it and *why* I thought about it. Doesn't it hold that the honest simplicity of understatement in selling a customer face-to-face will help him to remember you?

Like most people who find a good place to eat, a good insurance man with whom to deal, a good automobile dealer with whom to trade, a good doctor, lawyer, barber, shoemaker, breadman, tailor, or friend, I found myself inside the Chicago restaurant that said, *"We Have A Good Lunch Today."*

I found a quiet, pleasant, and clean atmosphere. The service was excellent, the food substantial, and the management most considerate of the needs and desires of their patrons. I had a "Very Good" lunch that day and other days that followed when I returned to Chicago. Why? Because I'm as receptive to low pressure understatement and treatment, as many millions of customers are in this busy, clattering world of ours.

We all love to cheer at parades, root the runs in for the home team at the ball park, applaud a well-given talk. We like to relax while eating, watching a movie or a good television program, just as buyers like to relax while buying.

The circus is a wonderful place for Jojo the Dog-Faced Boy, fanfare, balloons, barkers, and pitchmen, all of the wonders of the world promised with every 25-cent ticket. Even overstatement is acceptable at the circus or the carnival because we expect it there. But high-dollar selling is serious business. High-dollar salesman are serious businessmen.

Successful low pressure salesmen inspire confidence by being wise enough to avoid overstatements, improbable promises, and fantastic claims for their goods and services.

In high-dollar selling, customers want the facts. They want the truth. They don't want to be buttered by exaggeration. That is why high dollar salesman stick to the facts, tell the truth, and shun false claims and overstatements.

Why Humility Is a Confidence Builder

Being able to understand how small we really are in this vast universe brings us that much closer to the true meaning of humility. It's like watching people from the window of an airplane as it is taking off. They get smaller and smaller until finally, you can't even see them.

Humility is modesty, a real friend-maker, the best sale-maker. Great leaders have it. Great business executives have it. High-dollar salesmen have it. Champions in sports have it. Great scientists, actors, musicians, and writers have it. It is born of maturity.

Being the "life of the party" doesn't mean you are a perfect host or that people will seek you out. More often, people say, "I had a good time, but wasn't Joe Doaks a terrible showoff?" Customers say—

- I wanted to buy, but he was such a smart aleck. He knew everything.
- He wouldn't let me get a word in edgewise.

- He knew all the answers, so I just let him ramble and then sent him packing.

- He tried to tell me how to run my business, so I just ran him right out of the office.

- Went to the ball game with him yesterday. He pitched, caught, coached, managed, and umpired. Never again!

- He brags so darn much, I can't even remember what it is he sells. I know I wouldn't buy it.

- I complained about slow delivery, scratches, and chipping on his new cabinets. Instead of offering to adjust my complaint, he began to brag about his kid brother's tryout for the big leagues. No more orders for him.

Modesty attracts good business, good customers. It is part of the powerful magnetism of silence. Most customers hate showoffs just as most people do.

When you display modesty in selling, customers will sell themselves faster. Because you are giving them a chance to play the leading role. People appreciate having someone listen to their opinions and gain from their judgment and experience. They want to be helpful to those who will listen to them. The time to give your opinion is when you are asked to give it. That's when you bring your sales knowledge and your own experience into play.

The modest low pressure salesman knows how to accept and appreciate suggestions and opinions from customers. His approach to good selling is: I'll discover something useful today that I didn't know yesterday and that I can use for self-improvement and more sales tomorrow. It pays to be humble and modest. It pays to listen and learn from others. Just as it pays to trust others if you want them to trust you.

How faith in others builds
confidence and trust in you

The willingness to trust others gains the trust and confidence you seek from them. Princeton's traditional "honor system" for examinations has withstood the real test of time. Newspapers lose very little with their "serve-yourself" stands. Restaurants operated with honor systems lose less than those using meal checks. The unwritten honor system in selling requires that you accept your customer on faith value—not face value. You must have faith in people, if you expect them to have faith in you and if you expect to sell them.

Faith may not move mountains, may not win sales success for you overnight, but it certainly keeps your sale in the driver's seat over the longer haul. Faith and trust in others help you build a better you. And you don't have to go to church on Sunday to see it in action, for it surrounds you all year round in everything you and other people do.

- Your *faith* in drama critics takes you to the theatre, or keeps you away.
- Your *faith* in book clubs, book reviewers, spurs you to purchase the book or ignore it.
- Your *faith* in puncture-proof tires reassures you when you're on the open, rough road.

Why you should forget the
"sign here" technique

Since you have this faith in critics, reviewers, tires, and other products and services you buy and use, shouldn't you exercise the same faith with your own customers? It isn't too surprising to a high-dollar salesman, but the fact is that many millions of dollars' worth of big-ticket merchandise, land and oil leases, real estate, and other goods and services are sold daily in this country with a handshake for a contract. High-dollar sellers and buyers have faith in one another. They know one another. They've been doing repeat business with one another. They are friends of long standing business association.

Please don't misunderstand, I am not trying to impeach the value of contracts, insured loans, credit investigations, and the like. This would be an attack upon the policy of many companies. I'm just pointing out that your faith in the buyer creates his faith in you and that many high dollar purchases are made "without signatures on the order."

"Sign here, Sir." "I must have your signature, Mr. Smith." "Sorry, Sir, but we cannot ship without your signature." Sound familiar? Do you do it? Well, you shouldn't, because it leaves you wide open for this selling death knell:

> "Look here, mister, (he's so angry he won't address you by name) if your firm hasn't got enough confidence in you to accept my order as being all right without my signature, I have no faith in them. You'd better do business with someone else."

He's so right! This "signature on the dotted line" business went out with silk stockings. If you are selling to wholesalers or retailers, you don't need their signature on the order. Not if they are listed with Dun & Bradstreet. Not if the local banks say their credit is solid. Not if they have been at the same old stand for a reasonable number of years.

If you've sold the customer and he is willing to accept shipment, his credit rating and reputation for honesty should be signature enough. The most important signature is the one he puts on his check in payment for your goods and services. In other words, write up the order, find out when he wants delivery, how often he would like you to call on him, thank him for his business, and make your next call.

Too many words and too much valuable time have been consumed by salesmen who are still using the "sign here" technique. Forget it; high-dollar salesman don't do it; low pressure salesmen don't do it. It's "old hat," passé.

Main Points to Remember About Building Customer Confidence in Selling

The best way to win customer confidence, trust, respect and friendship is to prove you are dependable.

You prove dependability by showing people you are as anxious to please, as you are to sell

Customer confidence cannot be bought. Remember:

1. You earn confidence by being sincere, trustworthy.

2. You'll make more new friends, more new repeat customers, through confident, satisfied users.

Breed confidence with considerateness

You can do this simply by creating a sales atmosphere of pleasure, convenience, and relaxation. Considerateness is rememberable. To be pleasantly remembered is the aim of all low pressure salesmen.

Build your own confidence

Reward yourself with sales knowledge, practical experience, and constant practice.

"Know well what you are talking about," and people will talk well about you.

Get to know your product, service, and company better. Get better acquainted with your market, competition, and your prospects and their buying habits. Through this knowledge, experience, and practice, you gain full selling maturity and self-confidence.

Design a navigation plan
to win self-confidence

Building and maintaining self-confidence is a continuing process, a job within a job. It strengthens your self-confidence constantly through practice. Remember:

1. Follow the activities of your local Sales Executives or Sales Managers Clubs.

2. Attend seminars in public speaking at local clubs or universities.

3. Attend more trade association sales and business clinics.

4. Subscribe to trade papers. Study them for good suggestions and pass their interesting current and profitable ideas along to your customers.

5. Read more business and sales books to remain up-to-date on merchandising and sales methods and techniques.

6. Rehearse your sales presentation in front of friends or family. Get their reaction, suggestions, ideas.

7. Become more active in local civic groups. Exchange views with others. Build self-leadership as well as self-confidence.

8. Advance faster by studying harder, working harder, practicing harder.

Gain confidence by winning respect

When you listen to others and respect their point of view, you earn their respect for your point of view. The customer comes first in this exchange of viewpoints. So you must listen to him, learn from him.

Remember, too, "overstatement" kills confidence; "understatement" like "We Have A Good Lunch Today" inspires confidence.

Appreciate the wisdom, experience, and ability of others

You can always discover something useful today that you didn't know yesterday and that you can use for self-improvement tomorrow.

You make these discoveries through humility, trust, and faith in others. Especially if you want their trust and confidence in you.

Don't destroy the confidence of prospects and customers by pushing them to pay, to sign, to buy.

The word or the handshake of a high-dollar purchaser is as gilt-edged as his high credit rating, his reputation, and standing in the business world. Trust as you would be trusted, and you will sell your way to success.

5. Timing the Low Pressure Sale

The secret of low pressure sales timing is your ability to say or do the right thing, at the right time, at the right place, in the right low pressure way. It makes no difference—personal contact, a phone call, a sales letter, the talk you give before an audience, or social conversation—they all depend upon skillful, well-organized and practiced timing.

Sales timing is the art of *studied* sales speed. It just doesn't happen by itself. Like all other good salesmanship qualities, it must be acquired through study, observation, planning, practice, and constant improvement.

When you have studied your own timing, observed it carefully in others, and put this knowledge into daily practice, you will discover why better timing can help you make a friend with every sale, a sale with every friend.

Low pressure sales timing is a fine art. It incorporates poise, showmanship, and the ability to listen and learn from others. It produces a selling grace of movement, speech, and mannerism. It enhances self-relaxation, self-assurance. More important, it helps to relax your customer, and, on that score, helps him sell himself faster than you could ever sell him; that is how all low pressure sales are consummated.

Low pressure sales timing also helps you develop the profit value of making promotional suggestions at the right time to high-dollar buyers of seasonal goods and services. In addition, low pressure timing helps you make appointments faster and give your sale a welcome change of pace.

With the right kind of sales timing, you can outpace and outsell your competitor, and you can gain greater respect, admiration, and more repeat sales. For when you use this vital selling secret, you will find that it spotlights you, your firm, and your goods and services, in a dramatic, pleasing, and profitable atmosphere of sales relaxation.

The slapstick comic who throws pies and squirts seltzer may get a quick laugh, but we seldom retain long range impressions of pie throwers.

The genuine comedian, a true student of practiced timing, is gentler, more subtle. He can rock an entire audience by the well aimed tilt of an educated eyebrow, the rolling of his eyes, the quiet, studied pause before the punch line. This is timing that sells.

Look at what Zazu Pitts could do with her hands; what W. C. Fields could do with a well timed sneer. Dramatic actors establish a timing trademark, as evidenced by Gary Cooper's slow, ambling walk; Joe E. Brown's slow-breaking, infectious smile. These are only a few of the timing traits of people in show business, known down through the years to all movie-goers. They sell themselves through timing.

The maître d'hôtel is not "affected." He is polished, suave, and smooth. Even plain, unsophisticated, unaffected guests visiting his cafe or restaurant are impressed by the charm and poise of his greeting. They admire the relaxed, smooth, and graceful manner with which he escorts them to their table. They admire the quiet skill and dexterity with which he personally prepares their tossed salad, their crêpes suzette. His timing is just right, just so. It is dramatic, impressive, remembered. It is welcome, mainly because it is relaxing. He has sold himself, the restaurant, the food, and the atmosphere through timing.

People watch a chef in the window of a restaurant as he prepares flapjacks, flips them up and over with a rhythmic, evenly timed motion. Maybe some people watch to see him fumble a flapjack in flight, but this seldom happens, if ever. He's too good at it. Remember, he's had lots of practice, so his timing is just right, just so. It has eye appeal. It attracts attention, admiration, customers.

Mickey Mantle meets the ball right on the nose and sends it right out of the park. This is his trick of timing. Acrobats, golfers, milers, boxers win when their timing is "on," lose when their timing is "off." In other words, knowledge, skill, and intelligence, in the theatre, in sports, and in selling, are of little value without the proper practiced timing.

When you employ practiced timing in your sales presentation, pause regularly to let the customer do most of the talking, pause to think before you speak, and pause to think before you write a sales letter, make a phone call, or make a serious decision, you are practicing the art of low pressure sales timing.

Pausing to think before you speak or act, gives your brain an opportunity to think better for you, because you are relaxing it. What you say and how you time the speed of your sales conversation determine whether you are rushing or relaxing the brain of your customer.

How to Time the Speed of Your Sales Conversation

Tempo is one of the most important facets of the timing art. Just as your voice should be modulated lower than your customer's voice, it should be timed a shade slower than the speed of his voice. In other words, don't compete with your customer. You make the tone of your voice slower, so he doesn't feel he's being outpaced, rushed to buy.

Timing the speed of your sales talk, pacing it with dramatic pause, letting the customer do most of the talking, gives you a better chance to find out what you're up against, more time to adjust your thinking to the buyer's needs. Then, when it's your turn to say something, you have a chance to prove that you really were a good listener by furnishing him with promotional ideas that fit his needs—sales suggestions that will help him sell your goods and services.

An evenly paced sales presentation, geared to smoothly timed sales highlight points, gives the other fellow a chance to follow you more closely, think about what you want him to remember. It's not how much you say that matters, but what he remembers that counts.

The best way to practice improving the speed of your sales conversation, and make it more effective, is to try out your sales story on a friend, a fellow salesman, or someone at home. Try it on them. When they tell you what they remembered, you will have discovered the highlight points of your sales talk.

Once you know what highlight points struck home, it is simple to eliminate superfluous words and phrases, concentrate more on your highlight points, practice the sales timing of these points in future presentations. This makes for more articulate, thought-provoking interest in the rhythm, speed, and pacing of your sales points and ideas.

Remember that to put your customer at ease, give him a chance to follow you more closely, and impress on him your highlights, you must make your sales presentation as smooth and flowing as the dialogue of book characters. Practiced timing is the answer. There is no short cut to this powerful sale-making quality.

How to Give Your Sale an Important
"Change of Pace"

The fast-talking salesman, the quick "operator," and the unplanned "deal" maker, never stop to think of a "change of pace" in their thoughtless selling tactics. By change of pace, we mean saying and doing things that put us in a favorable, attractive, and attention-getting focus—things that let the customer qualify us as good salesmen before we qualify them as good customers. This adaptability is a good low pressure habit to acquire.

Like an unusual plot in a story, a unique treatment in a play, a striking fashion in bathing suits, a window display, a foreign sports car, or, for that matter, anything at all that attracts special attention represents a change of pace.

In selling, breaking away from certain outmoded traditions, static or obsolete methods and techniques—keeping pace with modern, unusual and profitable merchandising ideas—gives the high-dollar salesman a change of pace. These new methods and techniques are being flavored with low pressure seasoning more today than ever before. The reason is obvious. Hurry, tension, and pressure can be de-emphasized profitably in selling if you use a low pressure change of pace in your sales timing. For example:

- The abundance of white space in an advertisement, a silent salesman, gives the reader more mental time to absorb the message. It is a change of pace from the average ad, which doesn't let the reader's brain get a thought in edgewise; doesn't relax the reader. The fact is, any message, written or spoken, sinks in faster when it is relaxing to the eyes, the ears, the nerves, and the brain.

- Change-of-pace timing goes to work when the high-dollar purchasing agent, or purchasing principal is brought by the salesman to the factory instead of being expected to invest thousands of dollars on the strength of catalog sheets and sales brochures.

• Change-of-pace timing is often employed by high-dollar salesmen who arrange for a company-owned or operated plane to pick up the buyer, fly him to the factory, show him how the merchandise is produced, advertised, and marketed. Then, they get his order and fly him right back to his home town the very same day. Not every company has its own airplane, that's true. But at least those who do, prove how sales timing and change of pace are combined to keep ahead of competition.

• Bringing the appliance, furniture, or clothing retailer to the wholesale showroom fits a change of selling pace, fits a better timing pattern. The high-dollar wholesale salesman does it for several reasons:

First, he saves time by showing his entire line, demonstrating its quality benefits, its step-up structure. He could hardly accomplish this with a sample case or printed matter.

Second, the salesman now has an opportunity to introduce the retailer to the principals in his firm so he can see the caliber of business people they are, and discuss his credit and merchandise requirements with them.

Third, the salesman creates quicker confidence by giving the customer a first-hand glimpse of his company's method of stocking, shipping, and merchandising facilities.

Of course, if the customer is satisfied with what he sees, is confident in the principals,

their methods, and their products, and is handled in a low pressure way by the salesman,
the chances are he'll buy. He'll buy because
he has been exposed to a change of pace. He'll
buy because the salesman has brought him to
the right place at the right time, and said and
done the right things. Surprisingly enough,
there are thousands of distributors who, outside of periodic dealer showings, are not taking enough advantage of change-of-pace selling. Those who do it the high-dollar way, by
constantly refreshing their change of pace
with new ideas, new techniques, unusual but
practical methods, are well ahead of time
when it comes to making more sales and more
profits.

• Some retailers use change-of-pace timing, too.
For example, many salesmen and proprietors
of appliance, home furnishings, and piano
stores chauffeur customers to and from their
homes. This saves the salesman's time, the
store's time, and the customer's time. It eliminates the bother of traffic and parking for the
customer, places the customer in a more relaxed buying frame of mind. It is a change of
pace, because it is something most of their
competitors aren't doing. For that reason, it
gives them a merchandising approach that is
unusual. Of course, they wouldn't consider doing it unless sizeable figures were involved,
but these alert retailers know it is easier to sell
husband and wife or newlyweds when they
shop together. This way they avoid "I'd like
to talk it over with my husband," or "I'd like
to have my wife see it first."

How Timing Helps You Merchandise Your Way
To Sales Success

The high-dollar salesman uses the proper timing in many ways to merchandise his selling minutes. He uses the right timing in making appointments, instead of fidgeting in reception rooms until the buyer's secretary says, "Sorry, but Mr. Brown never sees anyone without an appointment."

High-dollar selling differs considerably from doorbell-ringing. High-dollar selling is mainly done by appointment. When you shoot for business at the high-dollar selling level, there are many reasons why the appointment is an unwritten law.

Purchasing agents, department store buyers, buying principals in well-run modern businesses, small, medium and large, have eliminated the old-fashioned method of giving sales interviews to salesmen at all hours of the day, every day. If they didn't do this, buyers would never have time to open their mail, handle their correspondence, make business phone calls, or handle adjustments, complaints, and new customers. It is quite different today. They insist on keeping their appointment activity on a planned, scheduled basis, at their convenience—not yours. Remember, if you want to make time with a high-dollar buyer, do a high-dollar business, make an appointment. Time it for the buyer's convenience. If the time he picks doesn't fit your own schedule, ask him to set another hour, another day. This way you allow for previously set-up engagements.

Some salesmen put themselves over a barrel by trying to cover too much ground without time allowance. They never give themselves or the buyer enough time to discuss the sale without hurrying it. Here is such an example of poor timing judgment:

"Excuse me, Mr. Doaks, could I use your phone to call Mr. Zilch and tell him I'll be late for my appointment with him?"

Doaks may appear courteous, certainly he'll say, "Sure, go ahead," but he'll think the man's timing is out of whack. Such a salesman won't make too much time with Mr. Doaks, either.

Needless to say, the high-dollar salesman doesn't let his appointments overlap. If he should fall behind schedule, you can be sure he doesn't advertise the fact during a sales interview. If he must phone another buyer to explain a delay, he'll call from a pay booth. He realizes that timing an appointment, timing a presentation, and timing the discussion that follows so it isn't hurried and yet so it sinks in, are the keys to relaxing every sale he makes.

How to Avoid Selling Pitfalls

You cannot merchandise yourself, your product, or your service with any degree of sales success by making calls without appointments. You cannot make your call sink in by rushing it, expecting the buyer to make quick decisions. You cannot build confidence or relax the buyer unless you give him time to think. Likewise, snap judgment and decisions made before you give yourself time to think are all a part of hit-and-miss, not high-dollar selling.

How many times, for example, have you given yourself a mental kick in the pants because you were unkind to your brain? Didn't let your brain relax so it could think success thoughts for you? How many times have you spoken out of turn, interrupted the customer? How many times have you regretted saying something that froze the buyer in his tracks? Remember how the smiling muscles in his face grew taut, tense, then grim? Could it be that your timing was off? Yes, indeed, it could.

Even saying the right thing at the wrong time can get you into selling trouble. Quoting price, for instance, before you justify the quality, the benefits, and the conveniences of your wares, is an illustration of the poorest kind of timing in salesmanship. Discussing politics, religion, or any other controversial subject is all right among friends. But, certainly all wrong until you make a friend of the customer, know his likes and dislikes, and understand his nature better.

Being self-opinionated is a display of poor timing in or out of selling. People have little social or buying time for the guy "who knows everything." Customers like to know something, too.

Low pressure timing keeps you out of these sale losing pitfalls, because it conditions you to *think before you speak*.

As we said in the beginning of this chapter, low pressure timing trains you to say the right thing, at the right time, at the right place, in the right low pressure way. If you think before you speak, you'll master the whole secret of low pressure timing in selling. If you project your speech with poise, courtesy, and finesse, and take plenty of time to listen to others, your only competitor will be another high-dollar salesman; for these are the timing qualities *he* practices daily in selling.

This is why timing, which has been somewhat neglected in selling as a great force, a great sales motivator, helps you merchandise your way to sales success.

How Promptness Enhances Your Sales Timing

Being prompt in sales timing is part of saying or doing the right thing at the right time. Here, for example, are a few suggestions on promptness you might incorporate with your own timing habits:—

1. Whether you make the sale or not, be prompt to send a letter of thanks to the buyer for his time, interest, and future consideration. A longhand letter is better because it proves you've gone to extra trouble to be thoughtful, courteous, and in the case of not selling him, a good sport. Believe me, it works wonders in maintaining good relations and securing repeat business. It's also part of the low pressure change of selling pace.

2. Be prompt to furnish more detailed information requested by the customer. The longer you delay getting the desired facts, the shorter the customer's delay in purchasing from a more expedient source. A night letter, a day wire, a phone call, a postcard, an airmail letter, or another personal contact to please the customer or give him the answers, can lead to a long, profitable association.

3. Be prompt to handle a complaint. The high-dollar salesman handles the complaint, processes it afterward. More repeat sales, good will and better customer relations have been destroyed through poor complaint handling than for any reason in selling. Remember, the customer has the problem, not you. Solve his problem first, solve your own afterwards. Being prompt, pleasant, courteous, and sensible in handling a complaint will mean one less future customer for your competitor.

4. Be prompt in the delivery of your goods and services. This insures the success of your advertising programs, prevents loss of sales from customers who say, "Why is it advertised if you don't have it to sell now?"

5. Be prompt in getting your sales materials, displays, brochures, etc., into the hands of the

wholesaler and the retailer. These promotional tools are part of double exposure since they tie in with national magazine and newspaper campaigns.

6. Be prompt to set up counter and window displays yourself if the dealer doesn't do it, rather than let them collect dust and become obsolete in the warehouse or receiving rooms. Don't take for granted they'll be used simply because they were designed and prepared for display purposes.

7. Be prompt to brief your wholesale and retail sales, advertising, promotional, and executive personnel on forthcoming national advertising and sales promotional campaigns. Keeping them posted on all changes and new objectives helps to win the full support needed to produce a well-timed merchandising and selling program.

Why Preparation Is Important in Sales Timing

The entire merchandising concept of high- and low-dollar selling is based upon preparation as well as promptness in sales timing. National, regional, and local selling campaigns succeed when they are carefully prepared and tested in the field, just as high-dollar salesmen succeed when they give careful thought and preparation to the planning of a sales contact.

A sales call that is timed without preparation is like a television commercial with the announcer asking the viewer at 11:30 Sunday evening to hurry to his local drug store. Of course the store is closed, the proprietor asleep, but the undaunted announcer beseeches the viewer to get up and go. It makes little difference that there may be a snow storm, a gale, or a blizzard at the time. The smiling, studio-sheltered announcer tells you not to hesitate. Such poorly prepared timing makes the sponsor ludicrous, and people have little faith and less sympathy for ludicrous appeals. They have many more intelligent things to remember.

Another example of poor timing preparation—in other words, something that isn't ready for customer exposure— is the case of radio or TV commercials that invite the audience to participate in the sponsor's contest by sending in boxtops, labels, cartons, etc. The announcer explains the usual requirement of writing a letter in 25 words or less on "I like Spoofers because . . ." What's wrong with their timing? It's unprepared, lacks fundamental salesmanship. Many of these commercials don't ask you to try the product, taste it, serve it to the family, use it, tell your friends about it. They take all that for granted. They figure if you send in the boxtops, you must have used the product. They are not really selling their product. They are selling contests. All they want is boxtops and labels.

Why Timing Is an Important Part of Seasonal Merchandising

The high-dollar salesman merchandises his selling minutes by developing the profit value of making good sales suggestions, at the right time, with buyers of seasonal merchandise. Here timing is of utmost importance because seasonal merchandise, like air conditioners, dehumidifiers, apparel, farm equipment, electric fans, and lawn mowers, are purchased at the risk of the wholesaler and the retailer. Like his customers, the high-dollar salesman keeps his eye on trends, weather, economic conditions, local payrolls. Together, they discuss the timing factors that will control the size of purchase and sales movement to the consumer.

Last year, a prosperous appliance merchant in New England, received a shipment from his distributor of table-model radios. They were part of a new fall line, introduced by the manufacturer in July, delivered to the merchant in September.

Being an alert merchandiser, the storekeeper dressed his windows around the end of August with the new radios, streamers, special trims, and banners. When completed, the new display was truly a masterpiece in "silent salesmanship." The merchant was ready for customers. He was ready, all right, but his customers weren't.

For five long weeks the frustrated merchant couldn't figure out why people weren't coming in to ask about the new models in the window. Then, he tried a new approach. He placed large streamers across the face of the window, announcing a price reduction of 25%. When this failed, he became disgusted, located the radios on shelves inside the store and dressed his window with other merchandise.

Now, he made plans to sacrifice the whole caboodle at half price, by running an ad in the local paper, and sending out postcards. After all, half the price, he figured, would be much better than liquidating the radios at a loss.

But before the ad appeared, and while he still had time to cancel it, customers came in to buy the radios. His entire stock was sold in four weeks. Every single radio was sold at the full list price! What was the reason? I asked him the same question and this is what he said: "I guess my timing must have been off. My customers were just not ready to buy new radios in September." He was right, too. *Portable* radios get the big buying play from June through September. These are the months people are out of doors, on the go. New models in table radios for indoor use seldom start selling well until three or four weeks after Labor Day.

Thousands in wholesaling, retailing, and service organizations have discovered the importance of timing in merchandising their goods and services. There are thousands of high-dollar salesmen who practice sales-timing their advertising, their sales promotions, their seasonal tie-ins, their sales calls, their letters, suggestions, and ideas.

The moral: Knowing *when* people want to buy is as important as knowing *what* they want to buy.

Points to Consider in Building a Successful Sales Timetable

To be objective, practical, ingenious, and creative in high-dollar sales timing, you must built a selling timetable, operate on schedule. Otherwise, you will find your goods and services, your ingenuity and creative sales ideas, being outpaced in the race for the buyer's dollar.

Whether you sell farm machinery, industrial equipment, chemicals, or flowers for a wedding, being a "Johnny come lately" because you didn't establish a planned timeable lets a more alert competitor, one who uses a timetable, beat you to the sales punch.

A sales timetable, properly prepared, properly carried out, can very well be your most effective selling tool. High-dollar salesmen would be lost without it; manufacturers, distributors, retailers would find their businesses in shambles without it, simply because the entire concept of marketing, merchandising, selling, and advertising would tumble without a carefully planned timetable of selling.

The successful high-dollar salesman cannot afford to use hit-and-miss methods. His time is too valuable. He stays ahead of his competitors by making appointments first, sales calls afterwards. This way, he avoids such costly, time-consuming regrets as—

- "He liked my presentation, said my merchandise was O.K., but told me he'd just bought a carload from my competitor. If I'd gotten him on the phone two hours sooner, he would have given me the order."

- "The nerve of that guy! I drove eighty-four miles to see him and when I got there, his secretary told me he had left for the city to visit my worst competitor. Maybe I should have phoned first for an appointment."

Getting appointments and keeping them on time should be the first consideration in preparing your timetable. Getting appointments is much easier, too, when you explore the timing requirements of your market. Developing leads and contacting prospects to close sales, like casting the actors in a play, is done long before the curtain goes up. Remember, your competitor isn't waiting. He's beating the bushes, making every effort to beat you to the sale.

An interior decorator I know, watches the newspapers for announcements of the construction of new apartment house buildings. These are his sales leads. He checks the name of the builder, then phones or sends him a letter requesting an appointment.

Having done work for other builders, and contacted them at "blueprint time," he knows what to say, what to write in order to stimulate interest. Why does he pick "blueprint time"? After all, it will be a full year before the building is completed. As you will see, his reasons are excellent.

After getting his appointment, the decorator asks the builder to let him plan, design, and build the furnishings for the lobby of the building. He highlights the point that the lobby will be finished long before the rest of the building is ready for occupancy. He explains why a smartly decorated lobby will attract prospective tenants, serve as a showcase for the character of the building. He sells his ideas, convinces the builder, and outpaces his competitor.

Through the builder the decorator meets the owner and the rental agent, establishes more good will and better customer relations. In turn, these new contacts open other merchandising avenues.

The lobby, you see, is a minor matter of profit for my friend. He makes most of his money by meeting future tenants through appointments set up by the rental agent. Of course he gives the agent a fair commission on all of the contracts that are closed. Also, he manages to do such an unusual, attractive, and appealing job in the lobby that it serves as his best testimonial.

So you see, even "blueprint time" can be the right time if you're working with a planned timetable.

Timetable selling is practical and profitable at every selling level because hundreds of products and services are sold to timetable buyers. Automobiles and appliances, for example, are sold to timetable buyers who wait for new models before they trade the old. Supermarkets sell their foods to thousands of families who buy a week's supply each time they shop. Vacations are timetabled. Purchases of hunting, fishing, and sports equipment are timetabled. Fuel, air conditioning, as well as hundreds of other items are bought by a timetable.

The high-dollar salesman, selling to manufacturers, wholesalers, and retailers, plans his timetable in accordance with the buyer's timetable. For this reason, he must familiarize himself with his market. He must study its economic conditions, its rate of employment, and its rate of expansion.

He must keep tabs on retail and wholesale movement. Most Sunday paper financial pages, for example, list key city department store sales. It's a good buying barometer to watch. Bank savings, home building, business and industrial expansion at local selling levels are also factors that fit the high-dollar selling pattern, give you a better perspective when you prepare your sales call.

How Low Pressure Timing Helps You
Outpace Competition

Ask yourself how many jewelers, caterers, and photographers follow the announcements of engagements in local newspapers, and send letters, postcards, or make phone calls to these very logical prospects? Not too many. Why? They ignore sales timing.

How many insurance agents, furniture salesmen, and appliance salesmen follow the daily records of fires in their local newspapers, and call on the owners of the homes, stores, and buildings that have suffered fire loss? Not too many. Why? They ignore the element of sales timing.

How many life insurance agents, diaper services, and furniture salesmen follow birth listings in their local newspaper? Not too many. Why? Their timing is off. If they utilized their selling minutes, if they operated with a timetable, they'd be following up these leads. A single word "Congratulations!" would be a sufficient low pressure door-opener to the sale.

How many banks send depositors a note at vacation time to advertise the value of safe deposit boxes, and offer tips on what their depositors should guard against when leaving for a vacation?

Being well ahead of time always puts you ahead of your competition. In other words, the right time to develop leads, contact prospects, and close sales, is long before the curtain goes up. Casting, production, direction, publicity begin when the script is ready, not when ticket-selling starts.

Governor LeRoy Collins of Florida adopted a low pressure timing approach in selling the advantages and benefits of his state to top executives in northern cities well ahead of time.

The Governor's advisors would contact key executives

in business, finance, and industry, and invite them to visit Florida, meet with the Governor, and discuss the possibilities of locating their businesses in his state. When they *are* ready to expand, they will naturally think of Florida.

Main Points to Remember About Timing the Low Pressure Sale

The best way to time the low pressure sale is to study the art of saying and doing the right thing at the right time in the right low pressure way.

Sales timing is the art of studied sales speed

Timing doesn't happen by itself. It must be acquired through studying, observation, planning, practice, and constant improvement.

Build better timing with showmanship

You do this by observing other students of practiced timing in the theatre, in sports, in high-dollar selling.

Remember: The great exponents of timing in the theatre are not "affected." Their timing is the result of practice.

How to time the speed of your sales conversation

When you make the speed of your conversation slower than your customer's, he doesn't feel he is being outpaced, rushed to buy. In other words, don't compete with the speed of your customer's line of thought.

Prove that you are a good listener by furnishing your customer with promotional ideas that fit his needs, sales suggestions that will help him sell his goods and services. Remember:

1. When you put your customer at ease, you give him a chance to follow you more closely. Keep your sales highlights in mind.
2. It's not how much you say, but what your customer remembers that counts.

How to give your sale an important change of pace

Don't be content with outmoded methods and techniques. Build a better change of pace by keeping up with new merchandising methods in your industry. Use new sales techniques that will bring your presentation into attention-getting focus. Remember:

1. Any message written or spoken sinks in faster when it is relaxing to the eyes, ears, nerves, and the brain.
2. Merchandise yourself, your firm, and the principals in it by getting the customer to see how your company operates; let him visit your showrooms, meet your boss.

How timing helps you merchandise your way to sales success

Make full use of your sales contact faster by making appointments first. Remember:

1. High-dollar business is not doorbell-ringing.
2. Don't put yourself over a barrel by covering too much ground, fouling up your appointment schedule.
3. Time your appointment, your presentation, and the discussion that follows so it isn't hurried, so it sinks in.

How to avoid selling pitfalls

You do this by not speaking out of turn and interrupting the customer. You cannot build confidence or relax the buyer unless you give him time to think. Remember:

1. Even saying the right thing at the wrong time can get you into selling trouble. Quoting prices, for instance, before you justify the benefit of your wares, is an illustration of the poorest kind of timing and salesmanship.

2. Discussing politics, religion, or any other controversial subject is all wrong until you make a friend of the customer, know his likes, dislikes, understand his nature better.

3. People have little social or buying time for the guy "who knows everything." Customers like to know something, too.

4. Low pressure timing keeps you out of these sale-losing pitfalls, because it conditions you to think before you speak.

How promptness enhances your sales timing

Being prompt in sales timing is part of saying or doing the right thing at the right time. Remember:

1. Display promptness by immediately sending a letter of thanks to the buyer for his time, interest, and future consideration.

2. Be prompt to furnish more detailed information requested by the customer. This can lead to a long-range profitable business association.

3. Be prompt to handle a complaint. Remember, the customer has the problem—not you. Solve his problem first, your own afterward.

4. Be prompt in the delivery of your goods and services. This prevents loss of sales from customers who say, "Why is it advertised if you don't have it to sell now?"

5. Be prompt in getting your sales material and displays into the hands of the wholesaler and the retailer to tie in with national advertising campaigns.

6. Be prompt to set up counter and window displays yourself if the dealer doesn't do it. Don't take it for granted that they will be used simply because they were prepared for display purposes.

7. Be prompt to keep your sales organization up to date on your national and local advertising programs.

Why preparation is important
in sales timing

The entire merchandising concept of high- and low-dollar selling is based upon preparation as well as promptness in sales timing. Remember:

1. National, regional and local selling campaigns succeed when they are carefully prepared and tested.

2. High-dollar salesman succeed when they give careful thought and preparation to the planning of a sales contact.

Why timing is an important part
of seasonal merchandising

Knowing *when* people buy is just as important as finding out *what* they want to buy. Remember:

1. High-dollar salesman study their markets, get to know *when* people buy.

2. They coordinate this knowledge with their
   sales timing in advertising, sales promotions,
   seasonal tie-ins, sales calls, letters, suggestions, ideas.

**Points to consider in building
a successful sales timetable**

Because high-dollar buying operates on schedule, high-
dollar selling can only be successful with a timetable. Remember:

1. Being a "Johnny come lately" lets a more alert
   competitor beat you to the sales punch.
2. A properly prepared sales timetable can be
   your most effective selling tool.
3. Getting appointments is much easier when
   you explore the timing requirements of your
   market.
4. Remember the interior decorator and how he
   made "blue-print timing" the right time to do
   business.

**How low pressure timing helps
you outpace competition**

This is the aspect of timing that uses sales promotional
ideas that tie in with other unusual requirements of customers. Remember:

1. New business, new sales leads and more new
   business friends can be developed quickly
   through newspaper announcements, stories in
   newspapers, and trade publications.
2. You outpace your competitor by looking for
   these leads, planning your call and following
   through.

6. Developing the Low Pressure Sales Personality

Up to now, many people have been led to believe that salesmen must rate especially high in extroversion, dominance, and persuasion. I take odds with this point of view, and offer this low pressure concept to substantiate my position.

My definition of a low pressure sales personality is: The ability of a salesman to apply the gentle art of pleasing people and getting along with them. This is how you establish *good will*.

The United States Supreme Court defines *good will* as "the disposition of a pleased customer to return to the place where he was well treated." I'm sure you'll agree that you cannot high-pressure people to buy and please them at the same time. Just as we all know that you cannot use high pressure hit-and-run sales tactics to build repeat business.

Being friendly, patient, courteous, considerate, and above all, honest with people, are the attributes you must constantly develop, improve, and apply if you hope to acquire a successful low pressure sales personality.

In the highly competitive world of entertainment, men like Jack Benny, Perry Como, George Gobel, Jimmy Savo, Jimmy Durante, Robert Cummings, Robert Young, exemplify the lasting, durable quality of repeat business with their audience. They are forceful, not dominant. They are persuasive, but gently so. True, they are extroverts, but know how to blend gentleness with extroversion to make it pleasing.

At press conferences, or public appearances, men like Dwight D. Eisenhower present this friend-making quality in a whimsical, quiet smile, a pleasant twinkling of the eyes, which seem to reflect inner understanding of those who are watching or speaking with them.

It would almost be like saying that the gentle quality of a man is what makes him stand out among men. So it is with salesmen who build their personality from the gentle ground up.

Philip Morris Cigarettes won thousands of new friends on television, radio, and in the newspapers for a low pressure campaign, based upon gentleness. For example, one of their television commercials, backed with soft, soothing, pleasant music, went like this:

> Gentleness is welcome in everything we do,
> And modern taste demands it in a cigarette, too.
> Have a gentle Philip Morris—
> Made gentle for you.

What is the friend-making secret behind this approach? The copy? Not altogether. The soft and gentle background music or the singers? Not alone.

Let's take the lead line: Gentleness is welcome in everything we do. It touches a steady desire of the listener. It removes the listener from the loud, pushing and shoving atmosphere of other nerve-grating, shouting commercials. Its quietness, at the opposite end of the contrast range, is a most welcome change of pace for the ears and the nerves. It is low pressure friendly. It gets along with you because it satisfies your desire to be spoken to, not shouted at. It registers favorably because it doesn't bully you into buying Philip Morris Cigarettes.

This is the key to the code your own brain must devise and decode when you face other people to sell them your product or service. When you are gentle with others, they will be gentle with you. Being gentle with you, they will offer less sales resistance, more friendship. They will prove their gentleness by buying from you.

Why you should develop a low pressure sales personality

Morton Freund, Executive Vice-President of Lawrence C. Gumbinner Advertising Agency, said, in an American Broadcasting Company interview: "I think that American business and advertising men are learning that in a world full of tensions, where people are immersed in their own interests and problems, they can catch more prospects with honey than with vinegar. I think you will see more and more advertising making a bid for attention by amusing or beguiling people, and more and more selling through ideas and facts that lead people to convince themselves. In other words, we are coming out of the caveman era, when the advertiser tried to win his prospect by clubbing him over the head, into a more civilized period in which he will court him more gently, more pleasantly, and in more mature terms."

What better reasons could you have for being low pressure minded? We are leaving the mistakes of high pressure selling to those in our profession who wish to be left behind. There is a new parade, a completely new trend taking hold everywhere. Those of us who join hands now, in the sound, fundamental, and profitable ideas of low pressure selling will be on the march to new and greater selling success.

Down through the years, I have met many men in high executive positions—men at the head of large industrial and retail business firms. Many of them started out as salesmen and wound up presidents. Perhaps it is a coincidence that each one of them started his career with a low pressure blueprint. Perhaps it was a coincidence, perhaps not. But I can tell you this about them. Were you to pass them on a crowded street, they would look like the average Mr. John Doe. They are no different in appearance than the people they have learned to understand and listen to—the very same people who helped make them successful.

These men became successful because they were able to lead, not dominate. They were low pressure persuasive, able to get people to sell themselves on doing what was best for themselves. They knew how to get things done through mutual communication, understanding, and agreement. They spent most of their time listening to others, learning from others.

A successful low pressure salesman has *listening power*. The great American humorist, Josh Billings, once said, "Silence is one of the hardest arguments to refute." The nineteenth century English author, Sydney Smith, speaking of the historian, Thomas Macaulay, said, "He has occasional flashes of silence which makes his conversation perfectly delightful."

How To Get Along With People

Like myself, you've probably read a million words on this important subject. Having read a million, I should like to boil them down to three. The best way to get along with people—and this goes for family, friends, relatives, and customers—is to *listen to them.*

Forgive my repetition of a thought from an earlier chapter, but it fits here, too:

People are more impressed with their own voice than they are with yours. So, if you want to get along much better with prospects and customers, listen to them! Perhaps you've seen this happen in a sale (I know I have):

The customer is doing most of the talking. He is telling the salesman how his grandfather helped design the first typewriter, or the first vacuum cleaner. The salesman isn't bored. He is the perfect audience for each reminiscence. The customer is in his glory. After all, why shouldn't he be? Wasn't it *his* grandfather?

Suddenly, the customer realizes he has taken quite a bit of the salesman's time, and has imposed on his good nature, and says, "Oh, yes, I'll accept delivery next Tuesday. I've enjoyed *our* conversation immensely."

It has happened this way many times. It will continue to happen as long as we play audience more often than actor. Let the customer be the actor. After all, he's paying for the privilege.

We could explore many avenues of motivation. We could build a tremendous superstructure of confusions in our minds as to why people buy. We could go on and on interminably into the realm of why they buy what they buy, instead of why they didn't buy what they should have bought. I think the answer is quite simple: If you listen to people, you will get along with them and they will get along with you. Once this rapport is achieved, you can sell them the top of your line, the complete service.

Since a sale is always made in the mind of the buyer, not the salesman, we could logically say that it is the you, within yourself, that must decide how much listening you're going to do from here on out.

Again, it isn't important to concern ourselves with what makes people buy. We know why they buy. They buy for comfort, convenience, pleasure, utility. Why do they buy from *you?*

If we were to survey a group of customers, presently doing business with a successful low pressure salesman, and ask them: "Why do you buy from him?", here are some of the answers we would get:

I like him; he's courteous and considerate.

I trust him; he's truthful and never mispresents anything.

I have confidence in him; he never breaks a promise.

I believe in his merchandise; it has always served me well. I guess most of all I like him because he doesn't push people into a corner in order to get them to buy. Come to think of it, now that you ask, he's very easy to buy from, and easy to get along with.

How to become low pressure popular

Becoming low pressure popular is the simplest thing in the world. Every successful low pressure salesman I know follows this simple rule: *never ignore the customer*.

Dealing with customers is a fine art. You cannot ignore them and deal with them at the same time. Turn your back on a customer and you turn your back on a sale.

One telephone operator says, "Sorry, sir, they do not answer"—a polite, friendly, and gentle handling of your call. Another says, "No answer"—a quick, cold, empty reply that lacks the warmth of the first example.

On some long-distance lines, the operator greets you with, "Good evening, may I help you?" On others, the operator coldly says, "Yes?"

These are indications that some telephone operators, like salesmen, take their jobs seriously; others seriously impair their jobs.

Low pressure popularity can be achieved more rapidly if we develop the practice of being gentlemen first, salesmen afterward. Being a gentleman in selling, or anything else, takes more than a "pardon me," or a tip of the hat. It calls for courtesy, patience, and good sportsmanship. Naturally, there are other demands, but we should like to dwell for a moment on the more important factors.

"It costs nothing to be courteous"

These words appear on a framed plaque in the reception room of one of America's largest industrial firms. When I first saw them, they set me to thinking. Of all the things that help to make a salesman a complete success in his field, there is not one that costs him a single penny. Ambition, initiative, courtesy, loyalty, perseverance, cheerfulness, and gentleness—not one of these costs a red cent. These are the low pressure personality qualities of our own making. The fact is, if we have acquired their opposites, the power to change them is within our own control. We can do it in our heads without overhead. It's simply a matter of wanting to do it and doing it.

You may wonder why I chose courtesy as a major point in developing a low pressure sales personality. Let me tell you why. One of the chief complaints of customers at the retail level is the lack of courtesy on the part of salespeople. Customers are ignored. They get brushed off by salespeople who care too little about making a sale, too much about their pay envelope.

Recently, I *wanted to buy* a battery-operated tape recorder. When I inquired about it, the salesman told me, "It's very expensive." Not being content with this damaging bit of information, he added, "I had a man come in two weeks ago, and his face turned white when I told him the price."

This particular salesman wouldn't extend the common courtesy of showing me the equipment. Instead, he was discourteous, insulting, and a poor excuse for salesmanship. Naturally, I left in a hurry.

Of course, this doesn't mean that every salesman working in that particular store is an insulter. But it does prove that thousands of sales and profit dollars are lost daily in this country because the high pressure salesman, in his failure to melt the ice, breaks through and sinks beneath it.

The soft and gentle approach to friend-making in selling or in entertainment has always been a successful formula. By using the profitable benefits of the low pressure personality, you establish yourself as your own best testimonial for your product, your service, and your firm.

As a singer, and as a man, Perry Como typifies the well-balanced, gentle extrovert. By direct contrast, many comedians who dominated television in its early days, have now been swept away by their own flood of seltzer-squirting. Does this prove anything? I think it does. It proves that *Alice in Wonderland* will last much longer than Mickey Spillane and that the melodic tunes of Victor Herbert, Sigmund Romberg, and Irving Berlin will certainly outlive and outshine "Rock Me Baby With A Blackjack Beat." It also proves that low pressure selling will be more important in days to come, as it has been since salesmanship began.

To sum it up, a low pressure sales personality is recognized by the gentleness of its wearer. It makes for long range customer profits, satisfaction, and lots of repeat business from people who prefer to buy steadily from gentle salesmen.

How to make more profits
through patience

Like many other excellent qualities, patience must prevail as an important balancing factor if the salesman wishes to succeed. He cannot be a "poor loser." Once he flashes a "poor loser" signal, he introduces a sales paralysis from which he may never recover.

Let's be realistic. In spite of the "experts," there is no such thing as a sales therapy or sales technique that is infallible. There is no such thing in selling as the perfect method of obtaining the signature on the dotted line on a "right then and there" basis.

The customer may need time to make up his mind. He may ask the salesman to return three or six months later. He may say he is doing business with a personal friend. He may say that several other firms have been invited to bid on the order.

If the salesman is up against a situation like this, and says, "I think you're making a mistake," or, "You'll be sorry you didn't buy from me," or, "I don't understand why you don't want to buy now and save money," he has indicated a lack of patience and understanding. He has also shown himself to be a "poor loser." He has practically killed his chance of ever selling that buyer in the future.

Good sportsmanship
is good salesmanship

We could say that there is also a quality of good sportsmanship a low pressure salesman must have in order to retain friendship even if the customer has not made a decision in his favor. Sooner or later, through constant contact and following-up the customer on regularly scheduled calls, a salesman who is a "good loser" may eventually find himself a steady winner.

Putting the Sale into Candlelight Atmosphere

Just how do you put your sale into candlelight atmosphere? Does that mean you must wax romantic? Of course not. But if you have a natural, sincere warmth and a friendly liking for people, they will return your sociability in kind.

The moment you introduce friendship into the sale, the candle is lit. The moment you show annoyance to the customer, the light is snuffed out.

Many sales are lost in retail, especially in department stores, because the candle is never lit. However, where specialized selling skills and professional salesmanship are required at high-dollar levels, candlelight atmosphere is *the order of the day*. The sales presentation, the showroom, and the merchandise or service are dressed to the hilt; nothing is spared to make the customer feel that he is being wooed with the ardor of a Romeo for a Juliet.

I know an insurance salesman in Boston who uses a candlelight atmosphere technique that really pays off. Why? Because his sales talk travels on tiptoe. It is so well modulated that he's practically got his prospect hugging him to hear what he is saying.

When you can get your customer to practically lean on your shoulder to hear what you have to say, listen to your every word, you've got it made! It's a kind of "confidential approach," and let me tell you, I've *seen* him use it successfully. I think it has merit because you can always capture more interest and attention by making the volume of your voice several shades lower than that of your prospect or customer. This way, the customer's voice sounds more important and much better to him than the more quiet sound of yours. This is a human frailty that *must* be understood by salesmen if they hope to sell people.

Remember, if you let the customer drive the car, steer the ship, and take command, he will sell himself much faster and feel so relaxed about buying that he will tell all of his friends that buying from you was like buying in a candlelight atmosphere.

The secret of "togetherness"

When Eskimos rub noses, there is a silent but mutual understanding of "togetherness." When young lovers hold hands, the same feeling prevails. When the salesman acquaints himself first with the needs, problems, likes, and dislikes of his customer, he has discovered the secret of "togetherness" in selling. For these are the things that bring customer and salesman together.

High pressure "bait" advertising may bring a customer into a place of business where the high pressure salesman may try to "switch" the customer from an advertised "loss leader" which he says "has been sold out" to another more expensive item. He may succeed in the switch. His firm may get the customer's money but this hit-and-run type of high pressure trickery catches up. Eventually it leaves an empty store together with a cleaned-out proprietor. Hardly the profitable "togetherness" we're talking about.

"Togetherness" in selling is achieved through the simple, sound, and intelligent method of asking questions to discover what it is your customer needs, and why he needs it. Remember, we aren't talking about shaving cream or razor blades or shoe polish or a hundred-and-one other small items that are purchased on impulse, through self-service or vending machines.

Let's talk about something that fits the kind of personal contact selling we are talking about. How about a house?

What does a good low pressure real estate salesman have to ask his prospect in order to achieve "togetherness"? Well, here are a few questions:

How many people are in the family?
(He asks this to establish the size of house his prospect may be interested in buying.)

What schools do the children attend?

(He wants to know if they are of grammar or high school age in order to suggest appropriate, convenient school locations.)

Do they wish to reside in the city or in the suburbs?

(He asks because even the most simple questions create a feeling of customer confidence in his intelligent approach to their needs.)

Do they own or rent their present home?

(He wants to establish some idea of financial responsibility. He may even wind up by acting for them in the sale of their present property.)

What price range home were they seeking?
What type of mortgage and how much?
Do they want a ranch-type or two- or three-story home?
How soon do they plan to move into their new home?

We could go on with other questions dealing with such products as automobiles, insurance, paint, etc., but I believe we've established the general idea. The same spirit of "togetherness" prevails in the case of soliciting new business by mail, by phone, wire, or in person. Ask sensible questions. Let the prospect occupy stage center and your play will get rave notices.

It stands to reason that the best salesman in the world wouldn't be able to sell a five-cent package of chewing gum to a person who didn't like to chew. Therefore, before you try to sell your product or service, find out, by asking questions, what your prospect or customer likes and doesn't like; what he wants and doesn't want. Once you've done this, you've acquired "togetherness."

Is personality more important than intelligence?

According to some educators, personality qualities are considered more important than certain basic skills in getting and holding a job. In selling, especially today, I believe we should consider a well-balanced need for both personality *and* intelligence, without favoring one over the other.

Up to now, many sales managers have compromised in their selection of salesmen by favoring the better personality, rather than the better brain. This is a dangerous method of selection, in view of the fact that a salesman with questionable intelligence cannot depend solely upon a good personality. On the other hand, the man with a higher degree of intelligence could still improve his personality qualities and become a successful salesman. Intelligence quotients (IQ's) are fixed and never change appreciably. Attitude quotients, which I call "AQ's" are flexible; they can be improved.

What Is Your Sales AQ?

Here are 11 questions dealing with your sales *attitude quotient*. Give yourself 10 sales points for each "Yes." A successful low pressure score should equal 110 points.

Yes   No

DO YOU L-et the customer sell himself?
O-pen your sale with a smile?
W-in more customers by letting them have the last word?
P-lace patience ahead of pushing to make the sale?
R-eap more business by going out of your way to please customers?

E-nthuse others because you
yourself are truly enthu-
siastic?
S-peak softly, sell softly, sell
successfully?
S-ell with self-control to avoid
arguments?
U-tilize all your sales tools to
overcome sales resistance?
R-elax yourself to keep your
sale tension-free?
E-njoy your job by being pleasant, alert, and ambitious?

If you fall below 110, your sales pressure is
still too high.

Why long-range low pressure
triples your profit—and how!

The low pressure salesman with a long-range view always manages to remain in the high-income bracket. His
objective is repeat business from the same customers. He
establishes customer confidence through repeat satisfaction. He applies himself quite diligently to the following
sale-making characteristics:

1. He is patient, friendly, courteous, and sincere, is well liked by prospects, customers,
   business associates, and friends. He is not a
   noise maker, shouter, back-slapper, or dou-
   ble-talker.

2. He is quiet-spoken, mild-mannered, and
   even-tempered, for he knows that an argument with the customer is not the salesman's
   privilege. He steers clear of disputes with
   tact and diplomacy. He is an excellent listener. He realizes that the customer is more
   impressed with the sound of his own voice.

He explores the customer's likes and dislikes by asking questions.

3. He is honest because he knows that alibis and generalities are customer-losing substitutes for truth and fact in making a sale and a friend at the same time. He never makes a promise he can't keep, never breaks a promise he has made. He knows that the bookkeepers use red ink to register sales made with white lies. He never breaks faith with a prospect, customer, or friend.

4. He doesn't brag about himself or his company. He never talks about how big his company is. He knows buyers are more interested in "square deals" than square feet. He knows that the buyer's "yes" makes his company big, and that it is his job to come down to the buyer's size.

5. He is complaint-considerate. Knows that service, adjustment, repair and replacement all build customer confidence in his firm, his product, and himself.

6. He is courageous, not defiant. He knows the difference between nerve and brass. He separates the difference by using politeness as the divider. He is dignified, not stuffy. He speaks face-to-face, not down to people. He doesn't toss big words around.

7. He's a planner, not a hit-or-miss salesman. He saves time by setting up appointments in advance. He saves sales by keeping appointments on time.

8. He's an introvert if it suits the sale, and never competes with the customer. He lets the customer tell the funny stories, show the baby pictures, talk about his vacation. He's tact-

ful enough to let the customer have all the fun. Especially since *he*'s buying.

9. He knows how to be positive about benefits, comforts, convenience, taste, pride of ownership. He knows that every customer is bargain-minded, and that it is up to him to make the customer believe that quality is the biggest bargain in the world.

10. He knows how to use his winning low pressure personality with everyone in the firm he represents. This includes the switchboard operator, secretaries, clerks, shippers, and business associates who share in helping him move his goods and services at the purchasing levels.

If you measure the customer by his country club, clothing, or bank balance, be careful, or you might run into a situation like the salesman at an exclusive department store in Dallas. The customer, accompanied by her husband, who was dressed in rumpled, baggy work clothes, asked the salesman to show her a rather expensive mink coat. The salesman's smile changed to a smirk when he observed the shabbily dressed husband. He displayed the coat, but it was quite apparent that his heart wasn't in the sale. The woman said, "I'll take it with me," and her husband wrote out the check. It was Saturday. The banks were closed. The salesman phoned the Credit Department. They didn't know the husband or his wife. No, they wouldn't accept the check. The salesman almost regarded matters as they stood as a personal vindication of his first judgment of the customer. That is, he triumphed momentarily.

When "baggy" trousers was told they couldn't take his check, he scooped out a fistful of hundred dollar bills, and said, "Never mind, I'll pay cash." How was the poor salesman to know that "baggy" pants was an oil millionaire?

You cannot force, or pressure people to buy. You cannot get them to like you unless you are willing to like them in return. If you're antisocial, for heaven's sake, try prospecting in the desert for gold or uranium, but don't get into selling.

If you have a job-snob attitude, you're better suited for work as a chauffeur, butler, or doorman at some swank night club or apartment house building, but definitely not for selling.

Getting along with people, being friendly and courteous with them, serving their needs, understanding their likes and dislikes, and above all, making yourself easier to buy from, are the main things you must consider while improving your own low pressure selling personality. Of course, you've got to be a promise-keeper, avoid the job-snob attitude, and learn how to get along with your own associates, too.

If you can do all of these things, train your brain to respond effortlessly to friend-making characteristics, you might even be able to sell yourself on the idea of becoming a low pressure sales millionaire. After all, every man who ever made a million in selling did it that way.

To summarize this chapter, a low pressure sales personality can be developed more easily when we learn how human beings behave, and behave like them ourselves.

Main Points to Remember About Developing the Low Pressure Sales Personality

A low pressure sales personality can be developed more easily when we learn how human beings behave. You cannot force or pressure people to buy. You cannot get them to like you unless you are willing to like them in return.

**The best way to get along with
people is to listen to them,
never ignore them, and always
be courteous to them**

Good salesmanship is low pressure salesmanship. Remember:

1. You'll make more profits through patience.
2. You'll make more friends (and eventually, dollars) through sportsmanship.

**Put your sale into a
candlelight atmosphere**

You can do this simply by making your sale quieter. Your customer will lean towards you to hear what you have to say. It's the "confidential approach" that raises the caliber of your selling.

Remember, too, that "togetherness" is essential in the low pressure sale, and it is easily achieved by asking sensible questions that show you are working in the customer's best interests.

Maintain your sales AQ

Though your intelligence is stable and seldom subject to change, your personality is flexible. Check yourself on these points and seek ways to improve yourself here. Remember:

1. Let the customer sell himself.
2. Open your sale with a smile.
3. Win customers by letting them have the last word.
4. Place patience ahead of pushing to make the sale.

5. Reap more business by going out of your way to please customers.

6. Enthuse others because you yourself are truly enthusiastic.

7. Speak softly, sell softly, sell successfully.

8. Sell with self-control to avoid arguments.

9. Utilize all your sales tools to overcome sales resistance.

10. Relax yourself to keep your sale tension-free.

11. Enjoy your job by being pleasant, alert, and ambitious.

7. How to Organize Yourself for Low Pressure Selling

Travelling to see prospects and waiting for interviews consumes an estimated 38 per cent of the average salesman's time. Writing reports eats up another 12 per cent, and only 50 per cent is spent in actual selling.

In most cases, the salesman determines his own "salary." Therefore, the more time he spends selling instead of "talking," the better off he is. To him, talk is not cheap. To eliminate time wasters and futile sales efforts, the salesman must have some form of organized approach. Otherwise, he is selling in a vacuum. *Nothing happens in a vacuum.*

How important is self-organization?

A recent survey of three thousand American salesmen ranked 'self-organization' third in the order of the most important requirements of successful salesmanship. Since 'ambition' and 'enthusiasm,' heading the list, are intangible attributes, third place self-organization was the first *practical* requirement mentioned.

The question of sequence is not important. Successful professional salesmanship represents a carefully planned

117

chemistry of creative and practical compounds. The high-dollar, low pressure salesman blueprints his way to sales success by planning, organizing, and preparing himself for every possible sales situation which may, and usually does, arise in the course of a busy selling day.

Self-organization is like big-game hunting. Whether you hit the bull's eye or miss the target completely depends on the caliber of your ammunition, the accuracy of your aim, the steadiness of your rifle. Having the right bullet, the right gun, the right target, and the right aim, is just the same as preparing yourself properly to come home with a bag filled with the right sales orders.

Selling without planning and self-organization is like a salesman wearing a fifteen dollar tie, walking around with a hole in his socks. His prospects can't see the holes, because they're in the toes. But the salesman knows they are there. This discomforting knowledge robs him of the self-confidence he would feel if the holes weren't there.

If you were a doctor, you would diagnose first, prescribe afterward. But you would have to check temperature, blood pressure, and pulse to determine the facts needed for the right prescription. You would need all of the facts about the patient before treatment could begin on a scientific, organized basis.

If you were an engineer, you couldn't build a road, a skyscraper, a bridge, or a tunnel until you surveyed the site, blueprinted your plan, organized yourself to obtain the right materials and the proper construction specialists.

The same is true in selling—*no matter what you sell.*

No matter what your business is, you cannot save time or money, or expect to build customer confidence and repeat business unless you adopt and apply a time-saving, sale-making formula that will help you organize yourself for successful salesmanship.

Why Self-Organization Is an Integral Part of Low Pressure Selling

Constantly, throughout these pages, I have used the expression "high-dollar selling," "high-dollar buying." Now is as good a time as any to explain my reason for using these terms. The "high dollar" salesman is the man who sells carload lots of major home appliances from the factory or the wholesaler; the man who sells heavy industrial equipment, bulk chemicals, farm tractors, buildings, houses, high-priced automobiles, swimming pools, farms, hospital installations, commercial refrigeration and air cooling systems, and similar products with high unit costs.

Naturally, this type of selling calls for more intensive planning and preparation than you would expect of a salesman dealing with shoes, hats, or clothing. In each case, however, the basic fundamentals of good salesmanship are completely identical. The only real difference is the volume of business, the higher unit cost, and the greater delicacy of the high-dollar salesman's situation.

Of course, there is another factor. The low pressure high-dollar salesman becomes more successful because his self-organization provides a much greater profit opportunity to gain respect and confidence from a high-dollar buyer. Let's put it this way: The high-dollar purchasing agent is generally self-organized to purchase. Otherwise, he wouldn't have the job. Self-organization is what the high-dollar buyer looks for in a high-dollar salesman. When the buyer is satisfied that you have presented a well-planned program, organized yourself to save his time, as well as your own, he has more confidence in what you've said about your firm, your product, or your service. Here again, is a practical, profitable, and successful method of selling that doesn't cost you or your firm a penny.

**How fact-giving produces
interest, action, sales**

Most buyers base their buying decisions on all of the facts they can get about your company's products and its reputation as a reliable supply source. Therefore, in order to prepare for a successful sales call, you must set yourself up as a one-man "fact-giving" board. In order to give you a specific idea as to what it is purchasing agents look for in a salesman, here are the views of three men who buy for large industrial organizations:

R. F. Plimpton, Purchasing Agent for Electro Dynamic Division, General Dynamics Corporation, Bayonne, N. J., says: "A wise salesman sells for both today and tomorrow. In selling for today, well-informed salesmen who call on purchasing agents with specific sales proposals, and who stick to the point without time-consuming digressions, are always welcome. In selling for tomorrow, the sales manager himself can contribute strongly by pre-selling, training, and holding each of his salesmen. 'Back door' selling and frequent changes in sales personnel reduce that concern's confidence rating with the purchasing agent."

J. J. Summersby, Vice President, Purchases & Traffic, Worthington Corporation, Harrison, N. J., says: "We buy products, materials and services from thousands of suppliers, large and small. In our experience, the best salesmen are those who know thoroughly the things they sell and their application to our business. Our buying decisions are based on the responsibility of the supplier, the quality of product, its availability and service, as well as the evaluated price after taking other factors into consideration. From our viewpoint, the best salesmen make sure that all of these points are covered effectively."

A. J. Dickinson, Vice President in Charge of Purchasing, Virginia-Carolina Chemicals Corporation, Richmond, Va., says: "The salesman who gives complete service is the one who will stand out above the crowd. He knows his product and can make worthwhile suggestions concerning the maximum benefits that can be obtained from its use. He is alert to see that the merchandise is delivered on time and that its quality conforms to the specifications given. In addition, he feels a personal responsibility to see that the buyer is satisfied with the transaction. Such salesmen are welcomed by purchasing agents."

I don't think we have to explore the above testimonials too thoroughly to recognize that each one of these men has indicated that his chief interest is that of dealing with a salesman who is well prepared, self-organized, and in a position to prove his preparation by saving them time in presenting his story.

How You Can Fit into Your Prospect's Buying Plans

There are many more reasons why you must organize yourself in selling, especially in high-dollar selling. As you know, many large corporations make their purchasing schedule for a full year ahead. Often, there are as many as 25 to 50 or more people whose collective agreement is necessary in the final purchasing decision. The man or men you call on in these firms have little time for small talk, wasted motion, hit-or-miss sales presentations, disorganized salesmen. In other words, if you fail to come to them with a plan, they have no room in their plans for you.

A self-organized salesman is always welcome to a self-organized buyer. That doesn't necessarily mean you will sell him right then and there, but it does mean that half the battle is won because you have gained the opportunity to

tell your story, the chance to further your future association, the chance to explore the buyer's specific requirements, and most of all, the chance to show how thorough
you were in preparing your presentation. Naturally, he
will recognize your preparation as being in *his* interest.
Knowing this, he will eventually do business with you.

How preparation lights
your selling path

The Christophers, an organization dedicated to human
achievements in the interest of freedom, and the advancement of the arts and sciences, have a wonderful creed: "It
is better to light one candle than curse the darkness." In
selling, the same reasoning can be used to prove that it is
better to plan three sales calls by illuminating them with
preparation, than to make ten in the dark on a hit-or-miss
basis.

If the salesman wants quantitative coverage and is willing to sacrifice qualitative results, he is sticking his neck
out to achieve a one-shot dollar. The sale made on a selec-
tively planned, mutually profitable basis is more important
to a salesman and his firm than a sale made for the sake
of making a sale—any sale.

Volume that is obtained promiscuously, without planning, can be disastrous to the buyer as well as the seller,
especially if the volume creates an inventory problem that
will only block normal repeat business and reduce the rate
of turnover the buyer should enjoy under normal business
conditions.

Jumping around like a bunny rabbit may give you plenty
of distance, but what good is distance if, after traveling
faster and covering lots of unplanned ground, you find that
you made lots of sales calls, but came away with few
orders? For instance, how many times have you recorded
notes like these on your call sheets:

- Buyer on vacation.
- Buyer now with another company. New man will consider us.
- Couldn't see me today. Said try in two weeks.
- Tied up in meetings.
- Out in the territory.
- Liked our story but complained about delivery of last order.
- Wants competitive prices.
- Wants better credit terms.
- Wants a new advertising approach for his market.
- Promoted to new job in another department. New buyer too busy to see me.

Yes, how many times have you made a call only to find that you could have saved dollars, hours, face, and future by getting an appointment, presenting a more complete, rehearsed, and carefully planned sales presentation? To become successful in selling, in business, in teaching, in law, in medicine, or in anything we do where we expect lucrative rewards, it is up to us to recognize that the present and the future belong to those who prepare, plan, and organize their thoughts and actions accordingly. Luck is a negligible factor in the matter. Chance selling is profitless, drab, undramatic, and offers no real challenge to the self-organized, creative, professional salesman.

How to Get More Self-Organizing Hours

In a survey of fifty salesmen, I asked, "What do you do with your time on a rainy day?" They were all flabbergasted. Most of them said: "What can you do on a rainy day?"

Here are a few of the things they could do on a rainy day:

- Read up on the product, read trade papers, study competitive merchandising prices, features, advertising.

- Phone or visit prospects. This is something that they should do on a clear day if they have organized themselves properly to prospect for new business.

- Visit former customers to secure new leads. Doing this on a rainy day puts the self-organized salesman well ahead of his competitor who doesn't expect to find buyers on the job when it rains.

- I'm sure you'll also agree that buyers are generally flattered when you take the trouble to see them in bad weather.

Rain or shine is the time for planning, self-organization, and preparation for the future of your firm and yourself if you expect to share in the profits, improve your own position, and advance in the company. Below are examples of a few things you must do in all high-dollar selling, if you want to succeed.

A full year has gone by since I purchased my automobile. The salesman who handled the transaction had told me that he would like to interest me in a set of four puncture-proof tires. I explained that I would be gone for a month in the car on a trip to Mexico City, and would like to have him contact me when I returned. A full year has gone by. He has never bothered to contact me. He probably never bothered to write down a memorandum concerning our conversation. He has never sent a post card, or phoned to ask how I enjoyed the car. He ignores the kind of planning and follow-through that a salesman should use to become successful. I don't think I'll be too interested in dealing with him on my next car, for it appears that all he wanted from me was a commission—not my friendship or my respect for his "salesmanship."

There is a shoe store in my neighborhood. If the proprietor kept good salesmanship records, he'd know I had purchased a pair of shoes from him two years ago. Since that time, he has never bothered to send a post card, or telephone, or solicit any additional new business from me. Had he sent me a reminder, I would have purchased another pair from him, instead of buying them on impulse at Indianapolis several weeks ago between flights.

It is not my intention to single out an individual automobile salesman or shoe salesman and to try to condemn these men for not organizing their salesmanship along more scientific lines. The truth of the matter is that the butcher, the grocer, the appliance dealer, the haberdasher, and hundreds of others in all levels of selling miss out on more dollars when it comes to preparing themselves and organizing themselves to do a more profitable selling job.

Recently, I visited a meat-packing company in Pittsburgh. The owner was proud of his new processing and packaging equipment. The plant itself was modern and streamlined, geared to handle additional products and a greater business volume. All of this was fine. I considered him an astute businessman who followed modern trends. That is, I considered him so until he described his selling methods. They were traditional in the packing business. But strictly 20 years behind the times.

His outside salesmen had no planned itinerary, their territories were not scientifically organized for getting the true potential that existed. The men on the routes were both salesmen *and* bill-collectors, a practice that cut down the efficiency of obtaining the new business they could have gotten had they not been expected to collect bills.

Figures on population increases, new families, new home building were never made available to their outside men because no one on the inside was sufficiently well-organized to understand their value.

Advertising and sales promotion programs were never organized with a "theme" or prepared with sufficient marketing information for the best merchandising appeal.

The business was being done on a hit-or-miss, catch-as-catch-can basis. Small wonder that they say many big firms are getting bigger and many small firms are getting smaller. More and more each day, the reasons are coming into sharper focus. Big firms operate on a big-league, scientific marketing basis. Their salesmen are trained and conditioned to operate the same way. If smaller firms continue to ignore the critical need for modern selling, we may become a nation of supermarkets in food, clothing, automobiles, and practically everything else that is today sold through independent dealers.

How to plan a low pressure sales call

Back in the middle thirties, I was part of a small advertising agency. There were three men in the entire enterprise. Each of us handled his own accounts, wrote his own copy, made his own layouts, and solicited his own clients. In fact, each man did his own research and planned and presented his own sales presentations.

One of my "pet" methods of securing leads was to study various trade-paper advertising, note the layout and copy of the advertiser and the consistency of his insertions. I would then pick those ads whose layouts and copy seemed ripe for improvement. That's how I set up my prospect list.

While foraging through a chemical publication, I came across the ad of a maker of wire mesh screens used industrially in gold-mining, and in the manufacture of chemicals and pharmaceuticals. This particular advertisement lacked illustration, brevity of copy, and specific information pertaining to the product, its uses, and most important of all, its benefits. It even lacked an invitation for reader inquiries.

The first thing I did was to visit the public library where I asked for reference material on wire mesh screens and their industrial uses. I was given a half-dozen books on the subject, and spent three consecutive mornings reading up on my prospect's product. At least this gave me a surface knowledge of the product, how it was made, what it was used for, and who used it.

Step Two of my plan called for personal contact with several concerns in the area that were using wire mesh screens in their business. I visited a commercial chemical company, spoke with their purchasing agent and several of their chemists. Naturally, I explained the purpose of my call, putting it in the nature of a product survey that I was conducting in order to sell my prospect intelligently. My "survey" was given full cooperation.

Step Three of my plan was sending a letter to

the manufacturer of the screens, requesting an appointment. In it, I mentioned that I'd obtained field information that would be of great interest to him in future trade publication approaches. I got the appointment.

Step Four of the plan was calling on the prospect with a new layout, a new copy approach, and a complete report of the "survey" which had been conducted in order to prepare the new advertisement. I got the order.

Getting the order was much easier because of the planning that had gone into getting it. The client had said, "Anyone that interested in learning about our business, is entitled to sell us their services."

Of course, it is important to mention Step Five, which calls for keeping the sale sold with the right kind of follow-through. Here, service plus constant, diligent effort to satisfy the customer after the sale is made is the secret of continuing sales success. This means that even in the case of the wire mesh screen maker, it was our responsibility to keep up with changes in his industry, his competitive picture, his opportunity with new uses, new products, new markets, and new customers.

The factor of follow-through teaches us that selling is continuous and that nothing is ever sold unless it remains sold in the mind of the customer.

No matter whether you sell wire mesh screens, trolley cars, or toothpicks: like an architect, you must blueprint what you plan to sell and how you are going to sell it. I have always used a simple, easy-to-remember formula. It applies to every level of selling, whether it be from the factory, distributor, the jobber or the retailer. I call it the "4 E-F Formula." Here's how it works:

How the 4 E-F Formula Helps You Organize Yourself

1. E-xplore the potential.
2. E-valuate the obstacles.
3. E-xhaust the probabilities.
4. E-xecute the final plan.
5. F-ollow through.

E-xplore the potential

Before you can make your plan work the way you want it to, you must organize yourself to initiate the plan. You must explore the potential to be sure it is worth your time and effort. For example, there is a national organization called the "Diner's Club" whose members are entitled to use credit facilities in restaurants listed with the Diner's Club. Diner's Club sales representatives who follow the first rule of the 4 E-F Formula, explore the potential, save lots of selling time by knowing that their best prospects may be contacted at advertising agencies, public relations organizations, manufacturers' sales representatives, theatrical booking agents, and wholesalers' representatives. Doctors, for example, are last on the list of potential customers. Therefore, because he has explored the potential, a Diner's Club salesman knows that he will spend his time more profitably by contacting advertising agencies than by persuading doctors to buy his service.

To repeat, modern, scientific selling calls for the elimination of retrogressive hit-or-miss, one-shot methods. Whether you sell to an already established clientele, or beat the bushes for new business, you can bag bigger game, more sales and more profits, if you plan for the hunt, pick the proper caliber ammunition and aim accurately for the right target.

E-valuate the obstacles

You must evaluate all possible obstacles and objections that may come your way when you present your sales story. You do this by knowing first what most interests your prospect in your product or service.

Years ago, a friend of mine, who was the proprietor of a drug store, conceived the idea of marketing chocolate Milk of Magnesia. His reasoning was quite sound, because small children, who hated the unsweetened, metallic taste, would offer little resistance to a pleasant-tasting product such as this. He was so enthusiastic about the idea that he worked long hours in an effort to create the proper formula and get it on the market.

Finally, he succeeded in producing the product and made plans to bottle and merchandise it, only to discover after selling his initial sample quantities that the chocolate soured in the product within a period of four weeks. Had he evaluated all the obstacles, and thoroughly field-tested his experiments, he would have realized that the product was not ready for marketing. He would have saved himself many dollars in the purchase of manufacturing equipment, hiring salesmen and other investments necessary to set up the business.

Every obstacle must be evaluated before you can hope to present a sound, convincing sales story. Making an appointment, keeping it on time and simply repeating the same sales story that you told yesterday to another prospect isn't enough. Today's prospect may present a new and different problem, a new and different need. In other words, before you make the call, you have to tailor-make your sales presentation to fit a specifically different requirement.

E-xhaust the probabilities

When you have exhausted the probabilities, you are then like an attorney who is ready to face the jury with a summary of facts, and evidence. You are well prepared to handle obstacles that might otherwise throw you for the complete loss of the sale.

E-xecute the final plan

Now that you've done all these things, you're ready to execute your plan, put it into positive, concise action. This means that you have a complete program to offer, a well-balanced plan, a ready answer for objections. In addition to all this, you have indicated sufficient reasons why the buyer should respect you for your professional approach to selling. Men who organize themselves like this in the business world stand apart. They earn respect and confidence from customers who appreciate in others the things they themselves do to become successful.

F-ollow through

No golf swing is considered good without follow-through; few home runs are hit without it; and fewer sales remain sold without it. Follow-through means more than keeping in touch with your customer by telephone, wire, letter, or postcard, to find out if he's in the market for more of your merchandise. Follow-through means that after you've sold your customer, you are duty-bound as a high-dollar salesman, to help him sell his. This obligation belongs to the man representing either a factory or a distributor.

Being in the field, working out the destiny of your own territory, makes you the boss of this territory. It also means that the problems and the responsibilities of your territory belong to a mutual, sharing company: your customer and yourself.

In essence, you become your own market research department, your own copy-writer. You also accept the charge of being your customer's advertising and sales promotion counsellor, because his market may not fit the national program furnished by the factory. Therefore, you must know the market and the people in it. You must keep your ears tuned to the pulse beat of these people. Then, you must make yourself an ambassador of good will for your firm, help furnish your customer with ideas on better public and customer relations, help him get favorable sale-making publicity in the trade and local newspapers. These are the components of follow-through that help to balance the sales ledger.

The Main Points to Remember

Inside or outside, factory distributor or retailer, salesmanship calls for the same kind of timetabling that is used to run a railroad. Don't let your sales train jump the track by not having a carefully worked-out itinerary for your selling day.

Get into the good habit of keeping accurate, up-to-the-minute records of the calls you plan to make and the calls you have made. An excellent method of record keeping is to apply the following format:

1. *WHOM* did you see?
2. *WHEN* did you see him?
3. *WHAT* did he need?
4. *WHERE* does your firm stand with regard to his competitive requirements?
5. *HOW* will you follow through on your return call in order to make your customer feel you are trying to meet his needs?

Remember: self-organization and planning is what the successful, self-organized buyer looks for in a low pressure salesman. Self-organization saves you, your firm, the buyer, and *his* firm time and money.

Nine out of ten successful high-dollar low pressure salesmen ultimately get bigger and more profitable orders by first obtaining appointments with their prospects. A postcard, letter, telegram, or telephone call is certainly much less expensive than the hit-or-miss method of skipping around like a jack rabbit to get business.

Get into the good sales habit of using the 4 E-F Formula, a practical, streamlined, and scientific method of hitting the target with the right sales gun and the proper ammunition.

Remember: selling is continuous. The successful salesman recognizes that the signed order itself does not necessarily mean the sale has been successful. It is what you do after getting the order to keep your product or service constantly sold in the mind of the buyer; that means repeat business for you. You do all this when you apply the sensible sales law of follow-through. When you follow through, your customer recognizes that you regard selling as a sacred trust and this helps to build the confidence that is so necessary in a successful seller-buyer relationship.

8. Handling Objections
The Low Pressure Way

Anything that stands in the way of making the sale is a sales objection. It might be an unreasonable customer. It might be an objectionable salesman. It might be competition, credit, a previously mishandled complaint. For that matter, there could be any one of a hundred rhymes or reasons why the customer didn't buy. Whatever the reasons, it is a fact that even the most unreasonable customer, who has to buy from someone, can be sold the low pressure way through tact, common sense, and patience.

What is a sales objection?

Boiled down, a sales objection is a customer's reason or excuse for not wanting to buy. When you match his reasons for not buying with your reasons why he *should* buy, you have neutralized his resistance to buying. When you fail to match him, his resistance is still there. He is uncertain, dissatisfied. In this case, he'll buy from someone who can settle his doubts. In other words, you must completely satisfy the customer before you can sell him.

Usually, the first and often the only chance you get to satisfy the customer before the sale, is in your approach to the sale itself. If your approach is friendly, it will make friends. If it is creative, it will create sales. If it is reassuring, it will create confidence.

The most important part of salesmanship is the approach, because most sales are made or lost in the beginning—never at the end.

How You Can Avoid Objections and Increase Sales Through a Low Pressure Approach

A good selling approach also helps you to avoid objections—particularly a smiling approach, for I'm sure you'll agree that even a chronic grump of a customer has little cause to resist a genuine smile or a friendly greeting. At least I have found it so. I've also found that when the salesman matches customer grumpiness with his own grumpiness, the sale is doomed from the beginning.

A good approach in selling is like a well-practiced, well-developed "short game" in golf. You might be able to send your drives a mile down the fairway, but the real trick is to shave strokes by making your approach shots come as close to the pin as possible. Selling works the same way when your approach brings you closer to the customer; at the same time it brings the customer closer to you and your product.

A good low pressure selling approach means more than a pleasant salutation. It challenges your ability to be different, ingenious, as well as creative.

For example, the attendant I know at a service station uses a creative selling approach by wiping off the car windshield before coming around to ask how much gas, oil or service is required. This is the approach he uses with everyone. With him, it makes no difference if the motorist simply stops for directions. He cleans the windshield anyhow. And no one ever objects to the fact that the quality is good, and his service excellent.

At any rate, his sales boom, even though his products cost a few pennies more, because he puts the satisfaction of service into his sale at the very beginning—in his approach, where it belongs!

A dentist who specializes in children's work uses the perfect low pressure approach to avoid objections. Parents bring their children the first time to acquaint them with the dentist. No dental work is done during the first visit. This is indeed low pressure salesmanship in action. Not only for the children, but their parents as well. His approach is friendly, reassuring. Does this dentist charge for the first visit? Is he wasting a lot of time? To answer both questions, no. He's gaining relaxed and confident patients. In fact, he has more business than he can handle.

A Fuller Brush salesman gets his sale across to friend wife with this creative approach:

"Good morning, madam. How are you today?"

"Just fine, thanks. What can I do for you?"

"I'm from the Fuller Brush Company. We're introducing a new item. I'm sure you'll find it quite useful." (He holds up a cellophane-windowed package containing 3 toothbrushes.)

"I'm sorry, but we have enough toothbrushes."

"Oh, no, ma'am. These are *guest* toothbrushes. This package of three guest toothbrushes is something you should have just in case one of your overnight or visiting guests has forgotten to bring his own."

"Oh, I see. Well, that's a wonderful idea!"

I'm sure that when our creative brush salesman is being paid for the guest toothbrushes, he'll have his sample case open and be ready to sell other items. Remember, selling is continuous—from the approach to the step-up.

How the Switch in the Selling Game Changed the Nature of Objections

The fear of something new . . .

Fifty years ago, selling was like pulling elephants' teeth. In those days, most salesmen were taught that anything short of mayhem was forgivable if they wound up with the order. Incomes were low, markets small. Selling was more selective, less competitive. Most business was done on a cash basis. Automobiles, tractors, power tools, and home appliances were priced far out of average pocketbook range.

Obsolescence was just another word in a spelling bee. People made the old things do, because they couldn't afford new. The sewing machine had not yet replaced hand sewing. The horse held forth in front of the plow and the carriage, while the farmer and Joe Doaks snubbed the tractor and the car salesman.

In those years, every salesman used high pressure. You might say he had to, because selling was more like a war game between the customer and the salesman. Needless to say, the salesman lost more battles then because the odds were heavily stacked against him. He faced two major resistances from the average buyer: The first was a strong customer reluctance to part with his money for anything outside of the realm of absolute necessity. The second resistance was tougher than the first. It was *neophobia*—the fear of something new. For example, did you know that as recently as 1933, 30 to 40 per cent of our 125 million population didn't use a toothbrush? People were still afraid that brushing would scrape the enamel from their teeth.

It took a lot of high pressure selling to convince the farmer to change from manual to mechanized and electrical methods. Although the first Model T Ford made its appearance about 1908, it took almost seventeen years to convince the American public that the automobile was safe, comfortable, and necessary. By 1925 there were 20 million cars in a nation of about 25 million families.

The fear of something old . . .

Today, sales resistance has been replaced by a steady consumer demand. The fear of something new has been replaced by the fear of something old. Many of the old selling methods are as dead as the past—especially those saturated with the questionable theory that, "When you make a big enough pest of yourself, the customer will buy something just to get rid of you."

Let's face it. Times have changed. Buying habits have changed. Selling habits, though, haven't changed enough to keep pace with the times. Here is a bit of current history to prove that high pressure selling is passé, and completely unnecessary.

A recent survey shows people are spending 94 cents out of every dollar they earn after taxes. Excess of births after deaths is 50,000 every week. People are making more money and are in the mood to spend it. In 1929, the average family income after taxes was $3,195. In 1955, 52 million American families were averaging $4,955, after taxes. The word "obsolescence" is now meaningful in marketing because the old car and the old appliance are regularly traded in for the new models.

Not only do people have more money, but they have more time to spend it, more leisure to enjoy what they buy. For example, the Life Insurance Institute reports that 12 billion dollars are spent annually for leisure-time goods and services. People are living ten to fifteen years longer.

Technology, electronics, and automation have made it possible to manufacture production-line goods at costs well within the range of practically every pocketbook. True enough, our cost of living may be higher, but so is our standard of living.

Business credit and bank loans enable more than 4 million varied businesses in this country to expand their manufacturing and marketing facilities constantly. Installment buying, charge accounts, and other forms of consumer credit are encouraged. Nine billion dollars is spent annually to pre-sell the public through advertising and assist the personal contact salesman at the point of purchase.

In the past fifteen years, food sales have risen 270 per cent; automobiles, 300 per cent. Television, which had its commercial beginning in 1945, has become a 10 billion dollar industry. People have become two-car conscious. Air-conditioned homes, stores, offices, and automobiles are fast becoming standard equipment. Radios, hearing aids, television sets, and many other electronic products for home and industry will soon be made smaller, lighter, and more compact with the advent of transistors, which will eventually replace the current vacuum tube. Modern chemistry will continue to create new synthetic fibers, resins, foods, and biologicals. Air transportation will be speedier. New home building will continue to boom.

All this, and much more that could be mentioned, points towards a golden era for salesmen and salesmanship. We haven't begun to scratch the surface of the *existing* potential, let alone that of the future.

If you have felt that the last few paragraphs sounded like a pep talk, my reasons should be quite obvious. I hope the contrast is drawn between yesterday and today in selling. Years ago, salesmen had to hunt for customers. Today, especially in retail, the customer has to hunt for salesmen. Yesterday, the salesman's toughest competitor was the scarce dollar, the fear of something new. These reasons for customer resistance have disappeared, and have been replaced by a demand to buy and by the fear of something old. Is pressure needed to sell people who want to buy?

How to Avoid Blowing Sour Notes Through the Horn of Plenty

In the past 25 years, I have trained almost 50 thousand salesmen in person and on paper—in soft goods, ranging from sweaters, sportswear, hosiery, and diaper services, and hard goods, from wastepaper baskets to television receivers. In these years, I've covered well over a million selling miles in the field from the retail to the factory level. My personal history isn't important here; I've injected it to qualify the following observations I've made of salesmen in the face of obstacles:

1. *Sales are lost when the salesman side-steps a customer's objection by pretending not to hear it,* instead of facing it squarely with facts. Particularly competitive facts, because you must know as much about your competitor's product as you do about your own if you expect to sell in today's competitive race for the buyer's dollar.

2. *A negative attitude by the salesman, for example, can be a sales obstacle* because it stands in the way of making a sale. The salesman who thinks selling is tough finds trying to make a sale a lot tougher. Some salesmen don't realize their own negativeness. They are like the man who violently says he doesn't snore when he sleeps. Yet, how could he know when he's sleeping?

Some insurance salesmen have told me how tough it is to sell insurance. They say insurance, being an intangible, is not like an automobile, which can be forcefully demonstrated. Do I agree with them? No, I don't, because this is a negative approach to a problem created by the salesman, not the customer. There are 110 million insurance policies in force today, and the insurance business continues to increase. That's a pretty tangible picture in my book.

All of us might do well to remember that quality, prestige, and service are as tangible as the physical measurements of an ocean-going liner, and certainly as tangible as the ticket you buy to make a trip on her. In other words, any salesman who doesn't use all of the wonderful selling tools available to him today has a negative approach, and doesn't know it. In this respect, you might say that negativism is an error of omission, while being positive, well prepared, and equipped with all the sales tools is the shortest selling distance to the pocketed commission.

3. *A snobbish attitude by the salesman is a sales obstacle* —especially the salesman who tells the customer, "Of course, if you want something cheaper, I can show it to you." This salesman is usually an amateur, self-trained psychologist. He likes to type-cast every customer. He thinks he knows the "live" ones and the "dead" ones. He's usually right about one out of a hundred; the other ninety-nine customers never come back. He also likes to play at being "proprietor" in handling a complaint. For example, if the customer asks for his superior, he usually says, "He'll only refer you back to me." With him, the customer is always on trial. He arrests, prosecutes, and pronounces sentence. But never once does he realize that it is he, like all salesmen, who is on trial, and must defend instead of prosecute.

4. *Any attempt to be too clever is a sales obstacle.* You've seen this selling type in action. He likes to believe he has hidden comedy talent. But the joke is always on him, because he only outwits himself and loses the sale while he tries to be another Jack Benny. He is like the butcher who was asked, "How much is your calves' liver today?"

"$1.32 a pound, Madam," he replied. "It's as fresh as paint."

"My, my," said the customer, "that's awfully high. Mr. Brown, down the street, gave me a price of $1.23."

"In that case," said the butcher, becoming quite blunt, "why didn't you buy it there?"

"Well," replied the customer, "Mr. Brown said he was all out of calves' liver."

"Look, lady," the butcher wisecracked, "if I were out of calves' liver, it would only cost you 34 cents a pound."

A good butcher wouldn't try to be so smart. He would justify his price by telling the customer that his meats were worth a few pennies more because they were carefully selected prime cuts, that they carried the federal inspector's stamp, which he could show the customer. He would also mention that his calves' liver was worth more because it was more tender and tastier, and that he handled a better grade of meats because his customers wanted the best that could be obtained.

How to Handle "Tough Buyers"

At this very moment, thousands of salesmen are wondering why certain buyers they call on won't give them a tumble, won't open up and tell them why they won't buy. Usually, the report to the home office indicates that the buyer is too tough to sell; that he is unreasonable; that he won't listen to reason; that he is impossible to do business with.

As a rule, the salesman writing such a report is so discouraged that he'll use every excuse in the book to avoid calling on that particular buyer. Why? Perhaps the salesman doesn't welcome objections. Perhaps the salesman has unthinkingly done something to offend the buyer, and the objection is hidden from view in the buyer's mind.

No matter how tough the buyer, you'll stand a much better chance of handling and hurdling his objections when you know what they are, and you are able to neutralize them. We'll repeat an earlier point here: that tough, unreasonable buyer is going to give *someone* his business. Why shouldn't it be you?

There is a good reason for all of this discussion about tough buyers, and why their objections should be as welcome as the orders you get on a resistance-free basis. The reason is practical, because once you are able to handle the tough buyer, and the tough sales situation, the rest of your selling becomes easier and more enjoyable. It is like the ballplayer who swings two bats before he steps into the box, so the bat he uses feels lighter and easier to handle.

The secret of handling a tough buyer is a rather simple one. If he won't open up and tell you why he didn't buy, make it your business to discover the reasons for his resistance. How do you do that? The easiest and most direct way is to ask him. It is the quickest way in selling to improve your salesmanship, because most critical and demanding buyers are fine judges of a salesman's ability. They expect more service of salesmen, not a "deal" or a low-grade product. They want, expect, and are entitled to the kind of salesmanship that fits into their experienced conception of good salesmen. They want the same sincerity and respect they, themselves, are willing to bestow upon a salesman who measures up. They recognize a thinking salesman with ideas, who can match resistance with whole- instead of half-reasons, and who leaves platitudes, generalities, and half-facts to the half-salesman.

What are some "buyers' objections"?

I have asked buyers about some of their pet peeves concerning salesmen who create obstacles long before the sale begins. Here are a few of the reactions:

- "The price wasn't too high. The salesman's interest in handling our objections was too low."

- "He called on me in a Packard. But tried to sell me an Oldsmobile."
- "I really couldn't afford an annuity, but he pestered me for three months to buy one. Wasted my time, and his own."
- "He wrote my name with a Parker pen after telling me that Paper-Mate was the best buy on the market."
- "He expected me to buy my office furniture from his firm but wore no hat when he arrived. Is that the way for a salesman to call on a hat manufacturer?"
- "He gossiped about my competitor, so I clammed up and refused to buy. Why should I stick my neck out with someone like that? He'd probably go around and gossip about me."
- "He talked for thirty solid minutes before letting me tell him I was interested in better-grade merchandise. Something he couldn't sell me."

We could go on and on with more examples of sales obstacles that are introduced and stimulated by salesmen, but there are more important matters at hand. At least, we know that good salesmen welcome buyers' objections because they bring the reasons for their resistance out in the open. The buyer who conceals his dislikes may give you an excuse for not buying, but never a reason, unless you face him man to man, and ask him, "Why didn't I succeed in selling you?" Believe me, the toughest buyer will not only tell you, but he'll respect you for your courage and your honest desire to improve yourself in his eyes.

Sales resistance has been replaced by consumer demand. A lot of sales resistance today is manufactured by salesmen who fail to recognize that customers don't object to price, *unless they can't afford to pay a higher price.* And there is always a lower price range available. They don't object to advertising unless it is exaggerated. They don't object to a certain brand unless they've had complaints about it that have not been handled properly. Most branded, nationally sold products are guaranteed, and complaints about them are handled fairly and honestly if the proper people have been contacted. People enjoy the convenience of a charge account, but they'll cancel it in a second if the policy of the store no longer pleases them. This seldom happens, nowadays. What is left for them to object to? Only the objectionable salesman. No one I know after twenty-five years of selling, who used low pressure methods, has ever been called objectionable.

How to Handle Objections by Being Specific Instead of Half-Factual

Ask a leading question, in the low pressure way, and then follow up with lots of intelligent listening. There you have the quickest and most profitable method of handling the average customer's objection successfully. The reason is simple. Old selling techniques ask the salesman to qualify the customer by prejudgment, based on amateur psychological guesswork. *Low pressure selling lets the customer qualify himself for you;* lets him sell himself by occupying the largest portion of the spotlight. In other words, you can judge his needs much better if you let him tell you what they are, and how he wants them handled. In most cases, you'll find that by letting him drive, the road to the sale will be less bumpy. Just don't be a back-seat driver!

When the salesman says, "That customer always gives me a hard time," or, "He said the price was too high," or, "My product is competitive, but still I can't understand why I haven't been able to sell him," he is offering *excuses* not *reasons* why he failed to make the grade. Perhaps you think this is being a bit harsh, but don't misunderstand—we'll allow for unusual circumstances, and other legitimate exceptions. The salesman doesn't live who can sell everyone—we all know that. But what the *excuse*-giving salesman may not realize is the fact that he may have lost his sale by generalizing, instead of being specific when the customer says:

"Your price is too high"

This is the classic *excuse* used by the salesman who tries to sell by the "price sheet" approach. In nine out of ten cases, when the salesman opens his sale with a price sheet, he cripples his opportunity to close the sale on quality. When he opens on price he seldom, if ever, gets the chance to justify the price by demonstrating the benefits of the product. Not only that: When he opens on price, he invites "It's too high," or, "I can buy it for less," and from there on out the sale has been sidetracked. Price becomes the paramount issue. John Ruskin certainly called the shot when he said, "There is hardly anything in the world that some men cannot make a little worse and sell a little cheaper, and the people who consider price only are this man's lawful prey."

Take my word for it. Keep your price sheet out of sight until you've talked and demonstrated benefits. If the buyer opens with "How much does it cost?" tell him, "I would prefer to tell you what it's worth and *why*, before I tell you how much it costs." If the quality is known, wanted, or expected, and you prove the quality with reasons, and with evidence of value, profit, turnover, advertising, and consumer demand, you need never worry about the price. A buyer convinced by tangible, specific buying reasons isn't worried about price, either.

The next time you face a sales situation where the price

angle threatens to sidetrack you, stop for a moment to reflect on this thought:

> If "price" were a bugaboo when the customer
> failed to buy from you, why wasn't it a hindrance
> with the customer you sold?

If you'll think about this, and remember what you said to other customers who bought without objecting, you will agree with me that good salesmanship is seldom handicapped by price objections.

Another thing to remember is that the quality of the product and the low pressure caliber of the salesman are remembered by the buyer long, long after the price is forgotten.

"Your goods don't have enough margin"

This is a typical objection bounced into the factory salesman's lap by the distributor, and into the distributor's lap by the retailer. Not enough margin. Not enough profit. It is one thing to tell a customer that he can make more money with your line. But it is like your trying to teach an eagle how to fly if you can't neutralize the issue of "not enough margin."

I have seen at least a thousand wholesale salesmen in action on this particular type of sales resistance. Truthfully, they flounder as soon as the customer hits them with the issue of margin, or discounting of prices. When the customer tells you that your margins are not long enough, he has given you the chance to talk about *turnover*. For it is the volume of business because of the rate of *turnover* that determines his profits today—not the margin alone.

The next time you are told that your margins aren't long enough, here's an answer you can give to neutralize this particular resistance:

"Perhaps our margins aren't as high as some of the lesser known brands you carry, but they aren't low, either. After all, we spend much more for advertising to build a greater consumer demand for you than the brands you're talking about. Your rate of *turnover* can be much faster and more regular. And this factor makes our margin better than competitive. It makes your profits better than competitive."

After you've made your point, show the customer your advertising schedule. Show him copies of current ads. Show him copies of ads that will be run. Show him figures that indicate the volume of space the product will enjoy in the newspapers, and in national magazines. These are your sales tools. With them, you back up your answers to resistance. Without them, you are like an out-of-tune violin in a symphony orchestra that makes discord of the harmony of all of the other instruments.

"I've got too many lines already"

This is a real dilly of an objection for the retailer to present to the distributor's salesman. He may use it at the beginning of the sale. If he does, try this question:

"Are all of your lines making the kind of profit you are entitled to in your business?"

Believe me, this question will get your sale started for you. It will give you the wedge you've wanted to get into your own profit story. He will tell you which lines are doing good. He'll also tell you about the ones that aren't doing so well. Perhaps he *does* carry too many lines. This may be his trouble. He may be investing too much of his capital for too little return. At least you have started the sale by asking the kind of question that gets the customer to do most of the talking. The right question, at the right time, asked in the right way, is a leading question that leads to the sale.

John Paterson, one of the founders of National Cash Register, told his men not to try to sell on the first or second call until they had asked enough questions to know how their products could best be used by the prospect. I'm sure he meant sensible, suitable questions. Questions, for example, that also start out with such phrases as "Don't you think that . . . ?" and "Don't you agree that . . . ?" "Wouldn't it be a good idea if . . . ?" This is a good question approach. It also gives you an opportunity to combine a suggestion with your question, as well as invite the opinion of the customer.

What Asking the Prospect for Advice Does to Clear the Selling Road

Even cold canvas can be turned into hot profits when you ask the prospect for his advice instead of being too quick to offer your own. Here's a story to prove it:

> "Mr. Jones," said the salesman, "I certainly appreciate this opportunity to show you my merchandise! But, I didn't come here today to sell you anything."
>
> The dealer was somewhat flabbergasted. "Why did you come?" he asked.
>
> "Well, sir," said the salesman, "people tell me you're quite a technician, and I'd appreciate your advice on something."
>
> Still mystified, the dealer asked, "What is it you would like to know about?"
>
> At this point, the salesman removed a technical diagram from his brief case. "Mr. Jones," he said, "my firm has just taken on this line of merchandise, and I'd like to leave this schematic drawing

with you, so on my next call, you can tell me what you think about the technical construction of this product. Would that be putting you to too much trouble?"

Needless to say, Jones was only too willing to be of help. In fact, after the third call, the salesman placed his entire line of television receivers into Jones' store. Not only that, Jones later told the salesman he'd decided to take on the line from the beginning because he was so impressed by the low pressure approach the salesman had used. It makes sense, doesn't it? And why shouldn't it? After all, it is a natural desire to like others better when they ask us for our advice, as it is to like others less when they give advice that is not requested.

How to Handle the "Contrary" Customer

Let us take an example of the neighborhood pharmacist who experiences the "contrary" customer, who comes in and asks for some shaving materials.

The "contrary" customer acknowledges his cheerful greeting with a muffled grumble and says he wants some razor blades. The pharmacist places a package of twenty before the customer. "No, no," says the "contrary" buyer, "just make it a package of five."

Now, our customer indicates he wants some shaving *cream*, states his brand preference and type. The pharmacist then places a large size in front of him. "No, no," says the customer, "make it a small size." And so it goes until the sale is completed. The pharmacist introducing large sizes of everything—blades, shaving cream, and aftershave lotion, the customer demanding small sizes because he is "contrary."

How should you handle a "contrary" customer? How should you meet a sales problem like this one the low pressure way? Here's the answer, not only for our pharmacist, but for anyone faced with the "contrary" retail customer, purchasing packaged goods. Next time you wait on him, say nothing. Simply give him smaller sizes of everything and watch him insist on the large sizes. Believe me, it never fails!

There are fifty thousand drug stores in the United States. How many more sales of higher priced items would they sell to regular customers who are stubborn about large sizes if they tried this silent low pressure sales technique?

Quietly applied, simple, effective, and fundamental psychological sales techniques are greatly needed in selling today. Especially when we are told that more than three billion dollars in extra sales in retail alone are lost because of high pressure selling and a lack of understanding people.

Use the Trade-In Angle When the Customer Resists Extra Value

The automobile salesman, for example, uses the trade-in angle in stepping up the customer to power brakes and power steering when the customer objects to paying more for extra features. The salesman says:

> "Next year's models will come with power brakes and power steering as standard equipment. Naturally, when you trade in your car it will be worth more then, because you invested in these wonderful features."

Of course, we expect that he will prove the extra foot ease and comfort of power brakes in the demonstration ride. Just as he will also prove how power steering means easier handling, turning, and parking.

The trade-in angle helps the salesman overcome the objection to the "extras" he is expected to sell. It should be used in selling appliances, furniture, homes, and many other items that are accepted on a trade-in basis.

This is another way of telling your customer about *all* of the value he gets in his original investment. All high dollar salesmen use the trade-in angle.

How the Competitive Approach Overcomes Objections

·With the human competition that goes on around us daily, I don't think anyone will register a single doubt as to how important competition is in the existence pattern. First of all, we need competition as a way of life to keep human ambition alive. We need business competition to keep our economy in balance by keeping prices at buyable levels. When prices go too high, spending goes too low and you don't need a large volume on economics to tell you what happens if that happens. We are geared to mass production and mass spending, just as we must face the unalterable fact that we must compete in selling or perish.

The beauty of all competition is this: when the chips are really down, the man with knowledge, preparation, and experience always manages to get his day in court. In other words, you can be pushed up to the top by others, or you can power your way to the top at the expense of others, but you can hardly expect to stay on top through the help of those you've pushed out of the way to get there. Getting on top, in other words, is not half as important as being able to stay there.

Getting to the top of your profession as a salesman can be most difficult if you're content to stand by and say, "Why didn't I think of that?" or "Why didn't I sell him?" The other fellow sold him because he thought of something you had evidently skipped or considered too trivial to mention to the buyer. Often, the reason behind successful competition is mental, rather than material. In other words, the good salesman sells an idea, a benefit, a value, instead of giving his merchandise away with a "deal" that isn't mutually profitable as it should be in good business.

Use the competitive "difference"

Practically everything that is sold has a competing counterpart. You never stand alone or apart on the firing line in selling. Your competitor, as George Romney, President of American Motors, describes him, "is the fellow who follows you into a revolving door and comes out ahead of you." That doesn't mean you have to push the other fellow out of the way, or be ruthless in your tactics. For some strange reason, the man who thinks foul or shoving methods are forgiven if they pay off, is like the guy who passes on the hill, and then passes into the Great Beyond. Competition challenges your imagination. If you have no imagination, or you refuse to exercise this God-given attribute, I'm sorry to say it, but you should try a less challenging profession than selling.

There is also something "different" about everything that is sold. The real trick is using the difference you have, to sell against what your competitor doesn't have. This is not a new approach. It is as old as time itself. There is nothing new under the sun. Yet there is always a new way to refresh a basic idea by giving it a fresh coat of paint.

The obvious or commonplace competitive approach doesn't stir the imagination of the buyer. You can always change the competitive pace by doing something for the customer that your competitor isn't doing.

How objections help you make the sale if you help yourself

One of the toughest customers I ever faced was a department store buyer who had attended a sales meeting given by one of our distributors for a dealer group.

I had just finished presenting our merchandise from the stage in the hotel ballroom when he approached, and said, "You factory fellows are all alike. You talk about how good your product is, how easy it is to sell, and yet, I've never met a factory salesman who ever sold a bag of beans to anybody at the retail level."

He didn't stop there, either, but kept on firing at me with both barrels, telling me how the market for higher-priced television sets had gone soft because of local plant shutdowns, how business was bad, etc., etc. When he finished, I asked him if he would be willing to display three of our most expensive receivers in his department if I agreed to put in a few hours of selling time at the store. He couldn't very well refuse because he had made the challenge and I was accepting it. At any rate, he agreed.

The following evening, I reported for work. It was understood that I was not to approach customers, but to wait until the buyer, or one of his salesmen, introduced me to a customer as a representative from the factory. From there on out, I was to be strictly on my own.

I was on my own all right. The buyer made sure that he was going to see some real fun. About 8:30, only 30 minutes before closing time, he brought a group of people over to my merchandise. I say a group because they were actually two families, who shared the same house. They had their children with them. As I recall, there were nine people, including the buyer. He introduced me, and then I went to work. At 10 minutes to nine, I had sold two identical receivers for $1,100, collected a down payment of $300, and made arrangements for them to come in the following Monday to pay a cash balance of $800.

How did I make this sale? I explained the reason for the receiver's front construction and design. I showed them how easy it was to operate by letting the children operate it. I showed them how they themselves could remove the glass in the front with a 10-cent Phillips head screwdriver to clean the dust from the tube face and the inside of the glass, thus saving themselves a 6- or 7-dollar service call. I slammed the doors to show them how tightly fitted and heavy they were, to protect them from warping. I turned on the picture and turned it off and turned it back on again to show them that it came into focus automatically. I played records for them through the set speaker system by plugging a record player cord into the phono jack attachment, and then demonstrated the tone control.

Why did they buy? None of my fifty competitors in the industry were selling that way. In fact, before I got through, the buyer had called over about ten of his salesmen to watch what was going on.

Before the store closed, the buyer shook my hand and said, "From here on out that's the way every man in my department is going to sell his merchandise." Before I left, he had placed an order for thirty sets.

The Moral: Do what your competitor isn't doing, and if it makes sense, you'll be doing just fine.

Main Points to Remember About Handling Objections the Low Pressure Way

You must satisfy the customer before you can sell him. Remember, most sales are made in the beginning—never at the end.

How the low pressure approach helps you increase sales

When you use a creative approach, you bring the customer closer to you and your product. Remember the examples of the service station attendant, the dentist, and the Fuller Brush salesman, and how they used a creative approach to put reassurance into the sale.

Why high pressure selling
has outlived its usefulness

People *want* to buy today. They have the money to spend and want to spend it. You can help them spend it by telling them why they should. There is no need to try to pull the money out of their pockets, or pressure them into spending.

Why consumer demand has
replaced sales resistance

Sales resistance has been replaced by a steady consumer demand. Remember, this is a golden era for salesmen and salesmanship. We haven't begun to scratch the surface of the existing potential, let alone that of the future.

How to avoid blowing sour notes
through the horn of plenty

The best way to handle objections is to face them with facts. Any attempt to side-step a customer's objection by pretending not to hear it puts a sour note into the sales music. Remember:

1. A negative attitude is a sales obstacle.
2. A snobbish attitude is a sales obstacle.
3. Any attempt to be too clever is a sales obstacle.

The best way to avoid being objectionable is to consider that *you* are on trial—not the customer. You must answer to the customer—not act like the prosecuting attorney.

Why good salesmen
welcome objections

Objections that are known instead of concealed in the mind of the customer can be handled, hurdled, and neu-

tralized more rapidly. Remember, even the most unreasonable buyer is going to give *someone* his business. Why
shouldn't it be you? Also, the best way to bring a tough
buyer's resistance out into the open is to ask him, "Why
didn't I succeed in selling you?"

How to handle price objections
by being specific
instead of half-factual

Customers want reasons, not excuses. They want whole-
facts, not half-facts or generalities. Remember:

1. The salesman with a "price sheet" approach
    kills his opportunity to close on quality.
2. Keep your price sheet out of sight until you've
    talked about and demonstrated benefits.
3. The next time you face a sales situation where
    the price angle threatens to sidetrack you, tell
    the customer: "I would prefer to tell you what
    it's worth and why before I tell you how
    much it costs."
4. The low pressure salesman and his product
    quality are remembered by the buyer long
    after the price is forgotten.

How to turn the sale your
way with "turnover"

When the distributor or dealer says: "Your goods don't
have enough margin," talk turnover. Remember:

1. It is the rate of turnover that makes the mar-
    gin competitive.
2. Prove your point with your advertising and
    promotional sales tools, used to build a greater
    consumer demand for your merchandise.

How to handle "I've got too many lines already"

When this objection pops up, ask the dealer if he's making a profit on all of his lines. The right question, at the right time, asked in the right way, is a question that leads to the sale. Remember:

> Combine a suggestion with your question to invite the opinion of the customer. For example: "Wouldn't it be a good idea if . . . ?" or "Don't you agree that . . . ?" This form of questioning invites the opinion of the customer, gets him into the act.

How to minimize resistance by asking the prospect for advice

Even cold canvas can be turned into hot profits when you ask the prospect for his advice instead of being too quick to offer your own. Remember how the salesman did it by leaving a technical diagram with one of his customers.

How the pharmacist handles the contrary customer

When the customer insists on smaller sizes in packaged goods, don't fight him, just roll with the punch. The next time he comes back, say nothing. Simply hand him the smallest sizes and watch him insist on the larger size. It never fails.

How to use the trade-in angle as a sales tool

Using the trade-in angle at the time of the original sale helps you step-up the customer. This is another way of telling the customer why his original investment has greater value. Remember how the automobile salesman used the trade-in angle to step the customer up to features like power brakes and power steering.

How to use the competitive approach against all comers

There is something "different" about everything that is sold. The real trick is using the difference you have to sell against what your competitor does not have, or to render a service that your competitor does not offer. Remember the moral: "Do what your competitor isn't doing and if it makes sense, you'll be doing just fine."

9. Highlight Closers in Low Pressure Selling

All selling is a promise. All good sales closes are based upon keeping the promise within the boundary of believability, and the claims you make for your product within the boundary of delivery.

The successful low pressure salesman, whose constant objective is repeat business from the same customer, knows *it is the promise he keeps, not the promise he makes that breathes the life of believability into the body of his repeat sale.* This is the long-range view of all good selling. It is sound, steady, and certainly has proved its worth since selling began.

The label on a package or a bottle is a silent sales close. Mennen's label, on its after-shaving lotion bottle, says, "Skin Bracer." It is Mennen's promise that the lotion will brace your skin after shaving, give it a cool, brisk, and refreshing pickup. If it fails to do this, you'll never buy it again because you would consider the advertisement of such benefits a false claim, a broken promise. Since millions of shavers use it, we can logically assume that it must be good, that it fulfills the promise, because millions like it. We can also understand why millions of people buy it repeatedly, as they repeatedly buy all leading brands of cigarettes, lotions, automobiles, insurance policies, and all other benefit-giving, reliable, quality products.

The salesman is part
of the sales promise

All selling is a promise. A promise to exchange your goods and services, and their benefits, for the customer's money. A promise to deliver these benefits in the form of more profits, more savings, comfort, convenience, pleasure, safety, performance, style, or beauty.

As a salesman, you are as much a part of the promise, as the products and services themselves. Obvious exaggerations, unprovable claims, meaningless superlatives, may get you one sale, but never a repeat from the same customer. There is no room in the selling profession for the man who attempts to repair a deliberately broken promise with a limping excuse. When your promises go out of bounds, your sale goes out the window, and lands with the dullest thud.

Selling is a promise, all selling. A sales or advertising claim is a closing promise. For example: "They Satisfy," is a positive statement but not of fact—at least, not until you yourself smoke them, and they satisfy you personally. Then, at least to you, the positive statement becomes a positive fact. So it is with closing the sale. If you tell the prospect you can save him money, it is only a promise. To deliver the promise, you must support your claim with positive facts in black and white where he can see your figures, and prove to himself that what you say is true.

It can be said that the salesman with a slick tongue comes a cropper when he meets a buyer with a slicker, sharper pencil. So, if you're out to prove a point while making an economy-appeal type of close, be certain that your pencil is as sharp, and as facile as that of the buyer.

The salesman, like the product or the service, is part of the purchase. He can be believed or discredited depending upon whether he wishes to sacrifice tomorrow's sale for today's "fast buck." There is no happy medium or short cut in the more profitable, long-range view toward repeat business. What you close on a fast, unethical sales today, is not as important or lasting as the repeat sale you open tomorrow from the same customer.

Why You Should Use the "Common Sense" Technique in Closing

A Texas millionaire had worked for many years as a bank teller in a small, booming oil town. While playing poker one night, he won the last pot which included several deeds to land then considered worthless, but used as cash by the hapless owner.

Four years later they struck oil on the "worthless" property. The teller collected seven million dollars for the deeds. He quit his job at the bank, and decided to go big game hunting in Africa.

He remained in Africa for a year. Upon returning, he purchased a ranch type home for an estimated 200 thousand dollars. Curious things began to happen. A contractor was hired to attach a small wing to the rest of the house. And, since the new occupant was a bachelor, the neighbors wondered why he needed more room.

When completed, the new wing rose up like a monstrosity. First of all, it looked exactly like a mausoleum. It was made of marble—about 20 feet high, 20 feet square. The neighbors then figured that that was where the owner expected to be buried. They fumed and fussed, and even threatened to seek an injunction.

Calm was restored, however, when the new neighbor explained why he had built his marble block house. Inside this most unusual shrine-like room there stands today a stuffed elephant. It's true—an elephant killed in Africa, skinned in Africa, stuffed in Texas.

Despite the enormity of the service rendered by a willing taxidermist, this story proves that he must have been a low pressure taxidermist, able to recognize that when a peculiar customer sells himself on a peculiar idea, you mustn't talk him out of buying your service—especially if he wants it, can afford it, and you are completely honest about delivering the service.

In the main, buying motives are sensible. True, some are foolish, impulsive, capricious and, in rare cases, even ludicrous.

Of all the *isms* in selling, business, and living, none is or ever has been more important than *fundamentalism*. By following low pressure fundamentals in closing the sale, we are in actuality following the line of least resistance, the line of good, common sense. There is little need to make selling complicated. Too many things are overcomplicated already, so let us keep closing the sale as simple as possible.

Let us look at closing this way: Before we can apply effective closing action, we must first understand the sensible, non-mystifying reasons for buying action. I have said "non-mystifying" because many motivation studies, clinics, and surveys are being conducted to "discover" what makes people buy.

Certainly we know that a man with a hole in his shoes, who can afford the price of a repair job, or a new pair of shoes, isn't too keen on walking around that way. So, we know what makes him get the repair job, or buy the new pair of shoes: necessity.

By the same token, we know why the family able to afford their usual, annual summer or winter vacation, pack up and go: pleasure and relaxation.

What do people
really want when they buy?

When you know the answer to this question, you have solved the first secret of closing the sale. When you know what people *really* want, you will tell them what they want to hear. You will use the appeal that pleases them most. Since time began, the basic buying motives of people have been geared to their basic needs. It is quite simple to understand. No matter what you sell, to whom you sell, put yourself mentally in the shoes of the customer and try to understand his reasons for buying, resisting, or complaining. Try to understand his obligations, his problems. Is this difficult? It shouldn't be, for he basically wants what you want when *you* buy. It's as simple as that. Figure out what you want when *you* buy, and you will have figured practically every basic selling close used since the first sale was made.

Every manufacturer is interested in specific buying highlights. But you must highlight the point he favors more than any other. If you investigate your prospect before you make the call, and analyze the needs and requirements of the purchasing division you intend to sell, you can determine the closing highlight well in advance. You can even get your appointment scheduled on that basis.

How to "highlight" the
"economy appeal" close
to sell the manufacturer

- The manufacturer wants his suppliers to give him the best quality components and service at fair, competitive prices.
- He wants and needs regular delivery.

- He wants and needs safe, reliable equipment to help him reduce his production costs, keep his lines moving.

BUT MOST OF ALL . . .

- His ears perk up when he hears you speak of *more profits, cost reduction, sales increases.*

- His ears droop like a spaniel's when you generalize, drift into small talk, platitudes. He hates time wasters.

- His eyes light up every time you mention *profits,* every time you mention *savings.*

- His smile becomes broader by the second when you can give him *facts and figures* to support all of the promises you have been making.

It is quite obvious. Your economy-profits closer with any manufacturer is the chief appeal used by trade-publication advertisers, in every sales letter or piece of direct mail he gets. When you close on more profits through more savings through cost reduction, you are telling the manufacturer what he wants to hear.

This is not a "story book" approach to closing. It is practical because it is based upon the common sense, uniform experience and good selling judgment used by all high-dollar salesmen. It parallels the same organization, planning, coordination, and action that goes into everything we do to become successful. For example, if you were the manufacturer, wouldn't you always want to reduce your costs, increase your profits?

Closing is simplified when you know what the other fellow wants to hear. Which sales point you enlarge upon, depends on which one interests the buyer most. What interests the buyer most is something you have to find out before you attempt to sell him. You cannot face him unless you are completely prepared to do so—prepared to use the selling benefits we have already discussed, plus those to come.

Let us review the closing benefits that appeal most to manufacturers:

1. Cost reduction, sales increases, more profits.
2. Quality components, materials, competitive prices.
3. Regular delivery and service.
4. Safe, time and money-saving business and production equipment.
5. Facts and figures to meet his specifications, support your sales story.

Here you have the five basic points to be found in the "Economy Appeal" close. Naturally, your sales presentation should include them all. *Cost reduction—sales increases—more profits*—those are the highlights.

**"Highlight" closing with the
distributor of retail products**

Boiling it down to basics, the distributor wants his factory to understand, consider, and furnish the following requirements:

1. A competitive pricing structure, containing adequate profit margins for his dealers, and himself.
2. A nationally recognized, uniform-quality product, backed by warranty, guarantee, replacement parts, servicing facilities, regular delivery.
3. Cooperative advertising and sales promotional support for the product and the service to

create faster turnover at the retail dealer level, build greater consumer acceptance.

4. Trade-paper and direct-mail advertising to prospective dealers for greater coverage, increased volume, more profits.

5. Sales and Service Training programs for his entire organization on a planned, regularly scheduled basis, conducted by you and your firm's service manager.

6. Balanced inventory, fewer liquidations, payment terms in accord with his financial capacity.

7. A more up-to-date understanding by the factory of his territory, its problems, potentials, and other marketing characteristics. Field assistance for his salesmen to open new accounts.

Armed with a complete understanding of these points, the factory representative does a better low pressure closing job because he is better able to confine his sales presentation to the "highlights" the distributor wants to hear. He is not just selling a product by itself. He is selling a complete program. He doesn't have to use high pressure when he can support his presentation with believable facts and figures. Moreover, his product may cost more because it is worth more. His program may cost more because it is worth more. But at least he can support his story with proof instead of platitudes. Remember, every distributor wants a complete package, a program. So, if you sell distributors, "highlight" your program.

How to "highlight–close" the retailer

Getting a dealer to buy new lines of merchandise, increase his current lines, give more display space, use more direct mail advertising, more local newspaper space, more outside selling, is no mean task for any distributor salesman. However, thousands of distributor salesmen, making the regular rounds of many more thousands of dealers, could close more sales in less time through "highlight" closing. Again, it is simply a matter of telling the dealer what he wants to hear. Most dealers want to hear these sales points:

1. They want and need a product that has strong acceptance, turnover, local advertising, a fair profit margin.

2. They want and need a product that has a known reputation for quality, minimum service and repair.

3. They want new, colorful products with attention-getting styles, packaging. They look for dramatic display, and promotional appeal. They want you to keep up with the Joneses too.

4. They want, and need your selling ideas on how to move their inventories faster, before you can expect them to buy more from you.

5. They want you and your firm's service manager to hold sales training and service meetings with their store personnel.

6. They want you to spend floor time with their salesmen, to show them how your merchandise should be sold to a customer.

Although every dealer, like every other businessman, thinks first of more profits through speedier turnover, he is swayed most frequently by Point Four—more sales ideas. So, highlight Point Four in closing retailers.

Why you should use the
"what to why" close at retail

As you've noticed, we've been coming down the marketing ladder to its very last rung—the retail customer. We started at the factory, to show that closing must be custom tailored to fit specific needs and requirements.

Basically, closing is the same with the retail customer, except for the fact that it's much easier to close at retail than anywhere else in selling. Why? Because 50 per cent of every successful low pressure retail sale is made when the prospect turns the door knob, goes through the revolving door, gets on the escalator.

An additional 25 per cent of the sale is completed when the customer tells you *what* he came to buy, and the remaining 25 per cent is taken care of when you tell him *why* he should buy it.

Using the *what to why* close, is the easiest way to separate the closing wheat from the chaff in retail selling. First, find out *what* your customers want, then tell them *why* they should buy it. Talk about the extra benefits they get from extra features. Don't talk price, talk benefits. Then, demonstrate the benefits.

Just think of how much easier the task is for the salesman in a department store when he tells the customer "This Lewyt Vacuum Cleaner is so light, so easy to handle, so easy to operate, you can hold the baby in one arm, do your vacuuming with the other." Then, to prove his point, he gives a live demonstration, although, perhaps, without the baby.

For some peculiar reason, the unimaginative, lethargic salesman, who regards selling as a contest, and the customer as an opponent to defeat, defeats only himself. True, selling is a challenge. It challenges your imagination, your ability to be creative, your ability to dramatize the benefits that people naturally seek when they buy. Selling is a pleasure because many people regard shopping and buying as an adventure. The low pressure salesman helps them enjoy this adventure, helps them select the best buy for their particular needs. He becomes a part of the adventure, part of the fun.

It's a fact. People enjoy spending their money for real values. Don't be ashamed to help them spend it. Don't be ashamed to ask for their money, either, for that is also part of the fun. Help them relax more when they're buying, by using low pressure, and they will spend more. The looser the grip on the pocketbook, the faster it opens.

Remember, when people shop, you are being shopped, as well as your product or service. You are a part of the purchase. In fact, you are the only one, who can set the stage, satisfy the audience, win good reviews for the entire relaxed low pressure performance. These are your retail *highlight* closers.

How to Give Your "Closing" a Fresh Coat of Paint

I think it is time we all faced the fact that "story book" closes, replete with resistance, stiff, formalized dialogue between customer and salesman, are as passé in selling as bustles. Sales techniques of years ago, with undue accent on the point that closing a sale is fraught with all kinds of objections, stumbling blocks, and word battles, are techniques that require a fresh coat of paint.

In ten years, our population will be increased by 25 million people. We will need more products, more services. Industries with vision have examined this new dimension, this new marketing potential. Their present plans call for immediate expansion to handle the increased demand to come. Selling will be competitive, but salesmen will not be resisted if they fit into the long-range, profitable trend toward low pressure selling.

Is there a specific moment
for closing the sale?

No. High-dollar closing starts when the sale starts. There is no timetable or rule of thumb for closing. Since most high-dollar buying is based on need, most high-dollar selling is based upon fulfilling the need. Being able to measure up to the buyer's requirements, create quicker interest in your story, attract dramatic attention to your goods and services, stimulate his desire to buy from you, and get him into the act of quicker buying, sums up the best attributes of the best closers.

"Story book" sales closes are too pat. They leave little room for the unexpected situation. In other words, the salesman who sticks too close to the book, often finds himself stuck with a "canned" sales approach. Young or old, the high-dollar salesman learns how to evaluate good suggestions from others, but to think and speak for himself in order to handle the unexpected.

You can make an
"opener" a "closer"

Here is an example of how a young, alert salesman made an "opener" a "closer" during an unexpected development in his sale:

> The buyer said, "I thought your firm would send us an older man to handle this sale."
>
> "It's true, sir, I'm only 22," replied the young salesman, "but after you see how easy it is for me to demonstrate this machine, you'll agree my age isn't important. This equipment will do my speaking for me. It will also simplify your direct mail problems, reduce your mailing costs considerably, and pay for itself within two years."
>
> The buyer was sold. Why? He had gotten a

logical reply to his first and only objection during the sale. Instinctively, the young salesman used this same objection to reinforce the positive, demonstrable benefits and economy of his equipment. Once he had done this, proved his "opener," by giving the buyer a full operational demonstration, the rest was simple. He made the sale. But he didn't make it at the end, he made it at the beginning.

Making "closers" out of "openers" is easier when you are prepared to back up your statements with facts, when you are positive in your approach, as well as humble, courteous, and sensible. But above all, be brief. Brevity is the most successful sales closer of them all. Let us say that when your "opener" (which is also your closer) is brief, your entire sales presentation smacks of brevity. The sooner you get to the point, the sooner you make the sale. That doesn't mean jet propelling *your* conversation. Remember, let the buyer do most of the talking. Let your merchandise speak for you. Let the buyer sell himself. That's the low pressure way.

How the testimonial technique makes closing believable

We could explore many rules and regulations for closing any sale, techniques for repeatedly asking for the order, trial closes, "story book" closes, etc. We could, but we won't, for ours is not a rules and regulations approach. High-dollar selling is much too flexible for a set of fixed "buy laws." To repeat an earlier remark from this chapter, all selling stands or falls on its structure of believability.

Keeping your sale at grass-roots level, or letting it go up through the chimney in smoke, depends on whether you are willing to develop the fine, low pressure art of sincere understatement, or fall into the trap of high pressure exaggeration.

Every high-dollar salesman knows he can be more believable, easier to buy from, if he uses the testimonial technique in closing. For instance, to a farmer, an inherently cautious buyer, he will say, "The new features I've described in this tractor will save you more time and money than the equipment you're now using. *But you don't have to take my word for it.* I'm sure if you contact Farmer Smith, who bought this very same model three months ago, he will back up every sales and savings point I've made."

The testimonial technique in closing has been used successfully in selling for several thousand years. It is an integral part of word-of-mouth advertising, the most potent selling benefit a product or service can have.

Of all the low pressure closes, it is the most effective because it symbolizes the thinking of others, the satisfaction of others, and the confidence that others have in your goods after buying and using them. Selling through others via the testimonial technique is not new; it is a selling fundamental.

Practically everything sold over the counter has been presold a hundredfold over the neighbor's fence. People sell and presell each other on everything they buy. Neighbors, friends, relatives all recommend automobiles, appliances, insurance, clothing, food, real estate, vacation spots, and what have you, to each other. Here, the word-of-mouth, testimonial technique is at work for every person in the selling profession. All the more reason why it should be used as a personal contact selling close.

I have two big reasons for bringing the testimonial technique into sharper focus. First, a testimonial helps you close faster, makes your sale more successful, more profitable. Second, if your competitor happens to be a high pressure salesman, a "one shot" boy, a "hit-and-run" salesman, he cannot use the testimonial close too. After all, what kind of testimony can you get from disgruntled customers?

It appears that the use of the testimonial technique in personal contact selling has been neglected. Not so with advertising in newspapers, magazines, radio, and television. Perhaps in physical selling testimonials have dropped out of focus because they seem commonplace, taken too much for granted. Whatever the reason, let us not forget to put the testimonial closing technique back where it belongs. At the top of the list.

After all, belief is born of confidence. Who can dispute that confidence is generated faster when you ask a prospect to consult a neutral, satisfied customer before making a high-dollar buying decision?

Why Step-Up Selling Is a Profitable Closing Technique

You can still remain in true, low pressure character, and step people up to higher quality and bigger benefits. That is why step-up selling is an excellent closing technique. It isn't so much a choice of which of two different models of a piece of equipment they buy, as it is *why* they should buy the unit with more features, more benefits, more durability, more comfort, more safety, more style and more uses.

Selling from the top down is a form of step-up, or sell-up selling. It makes closing easier since you have less chance to lose out altogether. Of course, this doesn't mean you should try to sell a Lincoln to a customer who can only consider a Ford. A high-pressure salesman intent on making a sale will attempt doing something like this, but never a low pressure salesman.

Car manufacturers, for example, make step-up selling comparatively simple for the car salesman. You can see, touch, and use these step-ups before you buy the car.

The internal mechanism of the motor, which is not visible, has been translated to horsepower. The demonstration ride brings the horsepower, power steering, and power brakes, into focus as step-up benefits. The extra surge of increased horsepower from eight instead of six cylinders, lets the customer feel the extra power step-up.

Examining the extra chrome and feeling the new, smooth upholstering materials of the better car helps the customer sell himself faster. Calling his attention to the more powerful radio and more modern heater gives the customer a tailor-made look at what he wants to see, and many step-up reasons why he should buy what he sees.

Is this low pressure selling? Yes, because the product and its desirable step-up benefits speak for you. The customer sells himself faster. He helps you sell others by word of mouth. He recommends friends to you, mainly because you didn't push him into your order book, but let him sell himself instead.

There are 45 thousand automobile dealers in this country. Many of them claim they are not making a profit on sales. Many of them, especially in the larger cities, account for tremendous unit volume, but they too say profits are slim. Profits could be better if they used step-up salesmanship. Let's face it. The step-up-minded car dealers are doing a good job, making new friends, new profits. They aren't complaining.

The step-up-minded high-dollar salesman spends less time dickering at the low end of his pricing structure, more time concentrating on sales to people who want more, and expect to pay more for extra benefits. But don't expect to quote a higher price for your product or your service unless you can justify the higher price with unimpeachable figures, demonstrations, and testimonials. Belief is won through facts, not fiction.

A Word of Caution About "Short Cuts" to Closing

In your rounds, you've probably come in contact with many salesmen inclined to boast about "how I got to the president of the company and sold him."

This could be called the "by-pass" close. Someone in the company responsible for purchasing has to be by-passed if the salesman "got to the president." That same *someone* will definitely short circuit any future short cuts attempted by the same salesman.

Of course, there are smaller companies in which presidents insist upon making all final buying decisions. But it is always wiser and more profitable to close through the existing chain of command.

How low pressure in closing helps you avoid future complaints

Since selling is continuous, and keeping the sale sold is the most critical requirement of all salesmen, the subject of avoiding future complaints is an important one.

There are many instances in the life of a high-dollar salesman when his personal integrity is placed in jeopardy if anything goes wrong with the product or service. Although he doesn't deserve unfair criticism, he may even be accused of being a high pressure salesman.

Often, in spite of the salesman's innocence in a complaint situation, he gets the brunt of customer's criticism. But, in all cases, he *must* remain even-tempered, evenly dispositioned. Such episodes try the souls of the best-intentioned salesman. Especially when the complaint has been unintentionally brought about by the factory or the distributor.

In any case, the time to avoid future complaints and misunderstanding is when you close the sale the low pressure way. This is the time to tell the customer every-thing he should know about how to operate the product, how to maintain it for the best performance. This is also the time to explain the warranty, the guarantee, its serv-icing requirements.

By doing all this, you can minimize future complaints by 50 per cent. Relax the customer by means of low pres-sure, and you *make* your own selling future, under such ideal circumstances.

The Main Points to Remember About Highlight Closers

1. Keep closing within the low pressure bound-ary of *believability* and you'll keep closing more sales, keep making more friends, more repeat business.

2. Closing is a *proving ground.* State your case quickly, positively, honestly. Support your claims with facts, figures, demonstrations, testimonials.

3. Use the *common sense close.* Tell people what they want to hear. Hear *what* they want to buy. Then, tell them *why* they should buy it.

4. Manufacturers are mostly interested in the "Economy Appeal" close, which features *cost reduction, savings, greater profits.*

5. Wholesalers are "program" buyers. Close them with realistic promotional sales pro-grams.

6. Retailers favor *sales ideas.* Close them with ideas on how to move the merchandise you expect to sell and the merchandise you have already sold, but which is still in inventory.

7. Friendly, relaxed "highlight closing" opens pocketbooks faster. Helps you get to the

point, and make your point in less time, with more effect.

8. Low pressure closing is not a contest. At retail, 50 per cent of the sale is made at the doorknob.

9. Low pressure selling is fun for the retail customer. Shopping is fun, buying is fun. Get on the "good humor" bandwagon, and enjoy the fun with your customers.

10. Make "openers" into "closers" by letting your product benefits speak for you through demonstrations.

11. Use step-up selling to close. Sell more benefits, more value, more comfort, greater durability. Sell from the top at the start.

12. Avoid the "short cut" close in order to avoid sales that short circuit, backfire. Stick to the chain of command. That's the low pressure way.

13. Avoid future complaints by describing the true value and correct use of your goods. Be sure the customer fully understands *everything* he's getting for his money. Explain the warranty, the guarantee, operation, and maintenance of the equipment, the "fine print" in the contract for services.

14. Remember, low pressure closing ignores the fallacy of "price" or "deal" selling for a fast, quick, unprofitable sales dollar. It upholds the basic sales law of better selling for better profits.

When you close with better selling, your goods and services return higher dollars, higher profits, more satisfied customers. That is why a low pressure salesman is a high-dollar salesman.

10. How You Can "Tell It Faster— Sell It Faster" Through Low Pressure

The subject of speed in selling has been purposely saved for the last chapter of this book, because it represents the end thinking all of us must do to keep pace with the greater speed of present-day marketing.

All of the material in the previous chapters represents the preparatory thinking that should go into a low pressure salesman's make-up. Being prepared, you are now ready to *tell it faster—sell it faster.*

It is not impossible to be a low pressure salesman and still sell *faster.* In fact, more haste is made slowly than rapidly. This means that a low pressure salesman who eliminates waste motion, plans for repeat business, and steadily satisfies his customers is selling his product or service much faster than Hit-and-Run Harry, the high pressure failure, who eventually runs out of targets for his one-shot methods. It also means that low pressure selling is faster selling because more people sell themselves faster when dealing with low pressure salesmen.

Why Quicker Sales Are a Must

All of us know that during the past ten years our population rate has climbed faster. We know, too, that products are being made faster. Increased production, automation, and the trend toward the "supermarket" have accelerated the need for keeping up our salesmanship pace.

All of these factors, plus the high increase in competition for the consumer's dollar, mean that all high-dollar salesmen are being asked to sell more goods, and sell faster. That doesn't mean you have to jet-propel your own conversation. If the customer speaks faster, that's his privilege. But it isn't necessary for you to do so.

The best low pressure salesmen know that you can make more sales in less time simply by trimming down your sales story to the essentials that will move the prospect to buying action. Naturally, this includes the approach, demonstration, and close. Most busy people appreciate the salesman who *boils down the sales story before it boils over.*

If you are now ready to combine your own talent, creative and progressive thinking, unrelenting hard work, and enthusiasm with each one of the following "tell it faster" techniques, you'll find yourself going to the bank faster, and find your bank account growing faster.

How to Plan Your Appointment Approach

Phone it faster

The Bell Telephone System reports that representatives of a diesel engine company in Little Rock, Arkansas, make appointments with out-of-town customers in advance by telephone. Completed sales visits are up 20 per cent. The Chicago representative of 50 West Coast lumber mills uses the telephone to contact out-of-town customers and to follow up inquiries. In one year, sales have increased 65 per cent. A farm equipment wholesaler in Portland, Oregon, telephones out-of-town customers to thank them for their orders. Four of these calls, costing $4.60 brought $1,180 in additional sales. A Norfolk, Virginia, parts distributor now invites out-of-town customers to telephone their orders collect. In seven months, the plan has brought in $17,798 in sales. Sales cost: less than 2 per cent.

Remember, at least half of the success of your sale will depend on getting an appointment.

Lord Chesterfield said, "I recommend you to take care of the minutes, for the hours will take care of themselves." We can all do well to follow these wise words by boiling down our sales tactics and presentations to quicker minutes. Take newspaper, magazine, and TV advertisements: Just think how much "sell" they pack into a quick, persuasive message. Consider the telegram! Each of these is geared to hourglass, time-conscious selling.

Wire it faster

The President of the Ladies' Aid and Missionary Society of her church was away on the day when the church was burning the mortgage. She decided to send a telegram of greeting, and ended it with the word "Mizpah." The clerk asked, "What kind of a word is that?" "It's from the Bible," explained the sender. "It means 'The Lord watch between me and thee when we are absent from one another.'" The clerk shook his head. "All right, lady, I'll put it in," he said, "but you sure are cheating Western Union!" Cheating or not, you can be sure that the message was being wired faster!

Experiment. Try different telephone and telegraph openings. Then favor the one that seems to click most often. When you get your appointment, be on time. Let the customer be late, not you. If he's late, he already feels obligated to you. If *you* are late, he may feel irritated enough to find the first excuse for terminating the interview.

Write it faster

Suppose you've phoned and your prospect was too busy to listen, but asked that you send him a letter explaining your program. You can write it faster, and register faster in Paragraph One, by saying: "Your suggestion that I send you a letter briefly outlining the purpose of our forthcoming appointment is a good one."

You've praised him for *his* suggestion. Your compliment attracts attention. You've made him feel good. You opened the attention door to the rest of your letter. You're on your way to an appointment.

As a salesman, you must be as positive in writing as you are in face-to-face speaking. For example, steer clear of the expression "I *hope* we can get together," or "I *hope* you will consider . . ." It is much better to say, "I *know* you will consider this matter thoroughly." Even the small difference of a single word lets your prospect know what kind of salesman you are. Make him confident in you and your product when you're writing. Use words that compliment him, but with sincerity; that doesn't mean buttering him up.

Another good method to use when writing for an appointment is the question technique. For instance:

> "Would you be willing to match ten minutes of your valuable time to know how you can cut your sales training expense by 50 per cent and still get 100 per cent profitable results?"

Some may challenge this method by asking why you should give the prospect an opportunity to say "no" before the actual appointment? The logic is that any prospect who refuses to be interested in a proposition that promises savings and results is not a good prospect to begin with.

Therefore, in high-dollar selling, your chance of succeeding with such an approach is always good, because high-dollar purchasers are always open to new ideas or time- and money-savers.

Using these methods of telephoning, telegraphing and writing helps to soften the toughest part of making a sale: getting the appointment. How often have you said, or heard a fellow-salesman say, "If I could only get to see him, I know I could sell him!" It's much easier with hour-glass salesmanship. Build a mental hourglass. Boil down your approach. Build more profit steam for yourself by following the low pressure leaders who've discovered these secrets and are using them.

How to give a "command performance"

Most high-dollar salesmen will tell you that the sale is won or lost in the first five minutes. So you must be ready to present your sales story briefly, informatively, and dramatically. You'll know if your opener registers when the buyer tells his assistant or secretary he doesn't wish to take any phone calls or be interrupted while you're there.

Demonstrate dramatically and you will capture immediate attention. Remember, if you're not dealing with technical products and engineers, your customer is far more interested in what your product will do for him or give him, than its technical construction. Make your product "jump through a hoop," then watch his resistance melt.

Of course, a bridge-builder can't carry his product with him. But he can bring his prospects to a bridge he's already built. This is a form of demonstration selling that is more effective than showing the prospect a photograph of the bridge. A rug-cleaner can't carry his factory around with him, but he can still bring the prospect to his plant to see how the job will be done. Demonstration selling brings the automobile and truck business over thirty billion customer dollars annually.

If you're selling insurance, or any other "intangible," don't ever face the customer empty-handed. Use a dramatic chart or visual device, even a portable slide projector to show what benefits he's getting when he buys from you. Don't try to depend upon conversation alone. Especially when you can dramatize your sales story graphically with interest-generating props.

Trying to sell from a specification sheet, a simple line folder, or printed brochure is like selling from an empty wagon when compared to a dynamic, dramatic demonstration. The man who sells a small, unbreakable portable radio, proves his point quite vividly by showing the buyer how he can drop it from a height of five feet without putting a scratch or a nick in the plastic housing. Will this demonstration capture greater interest than showing the buyer a picture of the radio, and making the statement that it's unbreakable? I'll let you answer that question.

Selling by demonstration is telling it faster without the need for long sales speeches. The demonstration speaks for you. I believe that one of our greatest needs today, in every nook and cranny of selling, is the demonstration, in one way or another, of the product or the service at the point of sale.

Recently, an insurance salesman said to me, "My product is an intangible. I cannot demonstrate it like they demonstrate automobiles and television sets." My comment to him was, "I have here a blank piece of paper. Assuming it is an insurance contract, why couldn't you simply tear it in half and say to the customer: 'Which policy shall I sell you, the one that gives you only one-half of the benefits you should have, or all of the benefits I believe you'd expect?' " So you see, the man who sells an intangible can still use a demonstration to make his point hit home. Its simplicity may fool you, but it works, because it is more dramatic than conversation by itself.

How humor helps you
move your merchandise

There is a place for humor in selling. Wholesome humor is welcome. Practically everybody has a sense of humor. It is a low pressure device since the most bitter sales medicine can be poured down the buyer's throat while his mouth is open with laughter.

In 1948, the maker of an ice cream vending machine came to us with his most serious selling problem. His machine was easy to operate, the ice cream bars were functionally loaded and dispensed, storage space was ample, refrigeration excellent. The unit was attractive, easily located, and easily serviced on the location. The ice cream was of high quality, and his price was right, ten cents. The machine even made change automatically! Why, you ask, did he have a sales problem?

Prior to the introduction of this new type vending machine, other people had tried to introduce similar equipment. Unfortunately, those who'd purchased the earlier units discovered that the bars would stick in the loading mechanism, and jam the whole dispensing operation. The machine wasn't easy to service or operate. It would not maintain even refrigeration, so the ice cream would melt before being dispensed. In other words, the earlier unit was a flop, and the word got around, proving that bad news travels just as fast in selling, if not faster, than good news.

This meant we had to do a public relations and publicity job before we could start advertising in the trade papers, or contacting prospective buyers. Our publicity job to obtain good will, interest, and customers, began at the Philadelphia Zoo.

With the permission of the Zoo officials, I had one of the units delivered to the grounds where it was plugged in to an electrical outlet. We then posed a model, a lively and rather intelligent 3-year old chimpanzee named Pandora, as she operated the machine herself! The monkey was photographed inserting a coin, opening the door to the ice cream compartment, removing the bar, unwrapping it, and then munching away at the ice cream a mile a minute.

Humor, yes. But that's how we started the promotional sales ball rolling. Here was a machine so easy to operate, a monkey could do it! You can be sure, we played this sales angle to the hilt that year. Results: Well, the entire campaign, including public relations, publicity, trade-paper and direct-mail advertising, saw 900 machines sold at a gross of more than 900 thousand dollars. Here you also had a combination of the creative sales idea, a visible demonstration, and pleasant humor. Let's put it this way: Handled *sensibly*, humor helps you sell much faster than a "traveling salesman's" joke.

How to simplify your letter writing and make it pay off faster

At RCA-Victor we had an inventory of one million book matches adaptable for dealer imprinting and distribution to customers. We wanted to move them fast so we could start on a new design for fall.

So we sent a flash bulletin to sixty-two of our distributors. The following week our match book inventory was sold out. Why? We typed the bulletin in red. As a heading, we used "A Red Hot Item." We burned the bulletins on all four sides, and even let some of the charred fragments fall into the envelopes before sealing them. Simple enough, of course. It proves, too, that you don't have to have expensive, word-heavy brochures or mailing broadsides to get your sales point across. It reinforces the point made previously that buyers appreciate a sales story that is boiled down before it boils over. Busy executives, especially, have little time to read long-winded sales presentations.

Simple, effective ideas can be inexpensive, and yet more potent, more powerful, and more profitable when they are used to open the door to bigger sales.

Why slogans help you sell faster

We are a country of battlecries and slogans. We are geared to this type of product and service recognition. Many of our leading corporations have traveled down through their business years on the coat tail of their own slogan. Food, cigarettes, clothing, cars, insurance, industrials, and home furnishings are all represented with slogans that have identified them for multiple generations of Americans. "When It Rains it Pours," "They Satisfy," "Time to Retire," "Ask The Man Who Owns One," "His Master's Voice," "Next to Myself I Like BVD Best." These and thousands of other slogans represent proud badges of company and product identity. They are deeply etched in the tall mountainside of American industry. But even more, they reflect a symbol of permanence with the buying public. They represent a wealth of confidence placed in these products by people who've helped make these corporations great with their purchases. Yes, a slogan helps you sell faster because it has *already* sold faster.

There are times when we think lightly of small things like slogans only because today's mass marketing also calls for thoughts of bigger, more complex means of selling. I would like to suggest that all of us take a backward step so as to be able to recognize the importance of big little things like slogans.

If your firm has a slogan, use it in your letters, your wires, your postcards. Be sure to include it in your sales talk when you are extolling the name of your firm.

Like anything else that will help you get your foot in the door, your own slogan is a sales helper. And there are still other "tell it faster" helpers, other ideas. After all, ideas cost nothing, and selling yourself, your product, and your service can be done much faster when you contribute ideas to others.

The Life Underwriters Association of New York City had invited me to speak to a group of life insurance agents. During my talk, I suggested that it might be a good idea for a life insurance company to print its small children's policies in two colors—pink for the girl, blue for the boy. After I'd finished my talk, one of the agents approached me and said, "Do you mind if I send your suggestion to my home office?" Naturally, I told him to go ahead. It made me feel good to give him the idea. Again, I knew that the use of one of my ideas would one day lead me to a sale with his firm. That's what you call the long-range viewpoint in low pressure selling.

Why ideas help you sell faster

Selling your customers is one thing. Helping them sell *theirs* is creative selling, and the best way to utilize your sales minutes. So you must keep thinking of ideas that will help the buyer speed up his turnover, win good will from his customers, get the edge on his competition, cut his costs.

To do this, make suggestions. Show him what is going over elsewhere. Study the trade papers. Make time-saving, work-saving, money-making suggestions. Your doing so is a short cut to continued buyer interest. Ideas are short cuts, to be sure. They give you more time to cover more ground, because with ideas, you are able to convince your customer that you are first interested in helping him— next, in selling him. In my travels, I've often heard a good low pressure salesman begin his sales talk by saying, "Mr. Smith, I came here to help you first, sell you afterward." Isn't this the most sensible sales approach in the world?

How you make more calls by telling it faster

Here again, hourglass selling is important because it helps you find more time to make more calls. When you make more calls, the success percentages are in your favor. More and bigger commissions come your way.

Some salesmen prefer to give most of their time to "key" accounts. Sometimes they stack the cards against themselves by putting most of their sales eggs in too few baskets. When the baskets get broken, the "key" account type of salesman finds himself in a bit of trouble. Why? Because he spends so much time with "key" accounts that he has no time left for smaller, intermediate volume accounts, affectionately called "bread and butter" customers by many salesmen because they buy regularly, seldom complain, and are not as demanding as larger accounts. However, when the going gets a little rough for the "key" account salesman he wishes he'd spent a little more time calling on more prospects. Hourglass salesmanship helps you make all of your prospects and customers "key" accounts. With more keys, you open more sales doors. It's as simple as that.

How to get to know when to ask for the order

Asking for the order prematurely sometimes puts a cold damper on the hottest sales story, in spite of the fact that some "experts" will tell you to keep asking and asking and asking for the order. Let's explode this theory right now. If he's going to buy, he's not going to refuse you because you didn't ask for the order ten times. If he isn't going to buy, you could ask a million times and it won't change his mind. It's a case of timing. You must get to know when to ask for the order.

Never ask for the order until you've covered every planned sales point, answered your customer's questions factually and convincingly. Naturally, the sweetest music to any salesman is the customer's "yes." Don't spoil the music by playing ahead of the band leader.

If you're shooting for a sample or trial order, try this one: "If you'll *approve* this order now, Mr. Brown, we will arrange to credit you with a full cash discount against your next requirement."

If you're shooting for a full order, try this one: "If you'll *approve* this order now, Mr. Bigelow, I'll give it my personal attention until you receive shipment."

Don't ask them to *sign* your order. Ask them to *approve* it. It makes a low pressure difference. *Approve* is more gentle, more solicitous, don't you agree?

Why you should keep the sales door open

Suppose that you have done everything a low pressure salesman does to get the order. Suppose that your sales story left nothing for the customer's imagination. So you didn't get the order! That's life, and selling, too. Don't waste valuable time brooding about it. Did you leave the sales door open for a return engagement? That's important. Did you follow up your call promptly with a courtesy note of thanks? No? Well, you'd better pound that typewriter today!

Always leave the sales door open for another day, another call. Put the prospect on your mailing list. Follow up the first call with a second. Analyze what you could have said or done to make the first call a success, and then follow through with a more complete performance. That's how other high-dollar low pressure salesmen do it. Remember, even a 400 hitter doesn't powder the ball for a hit or a homer every time he steps up to the plate. But the fact that he never stops trying is the reason why pitchers fear him.

**The main point to remember
about this chapter is:**

Get to the Point

Customers appreciate a sales story that
is boiled down before it boils over.

Time Out for Meditation

Shhhh . . .

Appendix

Through Sales Executives Club membership comes the immeasurable benefits of concentrated group activity. Regularly scheduled, informative club meetings are supplemented by panel discussions, shirt sleeve sessions; sales conferences, clinics and rallies; educational programs, special community activities . . . all geared to raising the efficiency and stature of the sales executive and his profession; and to raising the economic level of the community in which he lives.

List of Sales Executives Clubs Throughout the United States

ALABAMA

Birmingham Sales Executives
 Club
Thomas Jefferson Hotel

Dothan Sales Executives Club
Grimsley's Club Room

Mobile Sales Executives Club
Hotel Admiral

Montgomery Sales Executives
 Club
Whitley Hotel

ARIZONA

Phoenix Sales Executives Club
Hotel Westward Ho

Sales Executives Club of Tucson
Santa Rita Hotel

ARKANSAS

Sales Executives Club of Little
 Rock
Marion Hotel

CALIFORNIA

Long Beach Sales Executives
 Club
Lafayette Hotel

Sales Executives Club of Los
 Angeles
Biltmore Hotel

Oakland Sales Executives'
 Association
Lake Merritt Hotel

Orange Belt Sales Executives
 Club

Riverside—San Bernardino
Rialto Hotel

Sacramento Sales Executives
Club
El Rancho

Sales Executives Club of San
Diego
San Diego Club

San Francisco Sales Executives
Association
Engineers Club

San Jose Sales Executives
Association
De Anza Hotel

COLORADO
Colorado Sales Executives
Association
Swiss Chalet

Denver Sales Executives
Association
University Club

Pueblo Sales Executives Club
Minnequa Club

CONNECTICUT
Bridgeport Sales Executives
Club
Stratfield Hotel

Hartford Sales Executives Club
Hartford Golf Club

Sales Executives Club of New
Haven
St. Elmo Club

New London Sales Executive
Club
Mohican Hotel

Sales Executives Club of Southern Connecticut
Stamford

Sales Executives Club of Water-
bury
Elton Hotel

DELAWARE
Wilmington Sales Executives
Club
Hotel Du Pont

DISTRICT OF COLUMBIA
Sales Executives Club of
Washington, D. C.
Mayflower Hotel

FLORIDA
Jacksonville Sales Executives
Club
Roosevelt Hotel

National Sales Executives of
Miami, Fla.
Seven Seas Restaurant

Central Florida Sales Executives
Club (Orlando)
Eola Plaza Hotel

Pensacola Sales Executives Club
Pensacola Country Club

Tampa Sales Executives Club
Tampa Terrace Hotel

GEORGIA
Atlanta Sales Executives Club,
Inc.
Dinkler Plaza

Macon Sales Executives Club
Pinebrook Inn

Savannah Sales Executives Club
Johnny Ganem's

ILLINOIS
Sales Executives Club of Chi-
cago
Morrison Hotel

Sales Executives of Greater Peoria
Pere Marquette Hotel

Sales Executives Club of Quincy
Stipp's

Rock River Sales Executives Club (Rockford)
Rockford Country Club

Sales Executives Club of Springfield
St. Nicholas & Leland Hotels

INDIANA
Evansville Sales Executives Club
Hotel McCurdy

Fort Wayne Sales Council
Chamber of Commerce

Indianapolis Sales Executives Council
Marott Hotel

Sales and Advertising Executives Club (South Bend)
Morris Inn & Oliver Hotel

IOWA
Sales Executives Bureau (Davenport)
Blackhawk Hotel

Sales Executives Club of Central Iowa (Des Moines)
Hotel Savery

Sales Executives Club of Eastern Iowa (Waterloo)
President Hotel

KANSAS
The Kansas Sales Executives Club (Wichita)
Lassen Hotel

KENTUCKY
Sales Executives Council (Louisville)
Kentucky Hotel

LOUISIANA
Sales Executives Club of Baton Rouge
Mike & Tony's

Sales Executives Club of Lafayette
Place varies

Monroe–West Monroe Sales Executives Club
Virginia Hotel

Sales Executives Council of the New Orleans Area
Roosevelt Hotel

Shreveport Sales Executives Club, Inc.
Washington Youree Hotel

MAINE
National Sales Executives of Maine (Portland)
Commodore Restaurant

MARYLAND
Sales Executives Council of the Baltimore Association of Commerce
Lord Baltimore Hotel

MASSACHUSETTS
Boston Sales Managers Club
Sheraton Plaza Hotel

Southeastern Massachusetts Sales Executives Club
Fall River & New Bedford

Sales Executives Club of the Merrimack Valley (Lawrence)
Andover Inn, Andover

North Shore Sales Executives
(Lynn)
Hotel Edison, Lynn

Berkshire Sales Executives Club
(Pittsfield)
Wendell Sherwood Hotel

Springfield Sales Executives
Club
Hotel Sheraton

Worcester Sales Executives Club
Bancroft Hotel

MICHIGAN
Detroit Sales Executives Club,
Inc.
Ft. Shelby Hotel

Flint Sales Executives Club
Durant Hotel

Grand Rapids Sales Executives
Club
Rowe Hotel

Sales Executives Club of Jackson, Michigan
Hotel Hayes

Kalamazoo Sales Executives
Club
Harris Hotel

Sales Executives Club of Northwestern Michigan (Saginaw)
Rex Bar, Bay City

MINNESOTA
Duluth Sales Executive Club
Duluth Athletic Club

Minneapolis Sales Executives
Curtis Hotel

St. Paul Sales Executives Club
St. Paul Athletic Club

MISSISSIPPI
Jackson Sales Executives Club
Hotel Edwards

MISSOURI
Kansas City Advertising & Sales
Executives Club
913 Baltimore

Sales Executives Association of
St. Louis
Hotel Statler

MONTANA
The Billings National Sales
Executives Club
(P. O. Box 1196)

NEBRASKA
Omaha Sales Executives
Blackstone Hotel

NEVADA
Sales Executives of Southern
Nevada (Las Vegas)
El Cortez Hotel

NEW HAMPSHIRE
Sales Executives Club of New
Hampshire (Manchester)
Chamber of Commerce

NEW JERSEY
Monmouth County Sales Executives Club
Asbury Park

Sales Executives Club of Northern New Jersey
Hotel Robert Treat (Newark)

NEW MEXICO
Albuquerque Sales Executives
Alvarado Hotel

NEW YORK

National Sales Executives of
Eastern New York
Dewitt Clinton Hotel (Albany)

Buffalo–Niagara Sales Executives, Inc.
Hotel Statler

Elmira Area National Sales
Executives
Langwell Hotel (Elmira)

Sales Executives Club of Long
Island
Garden City

Sales Executives Club of New
York
Roosevelt Hotel, New York City

Sales Executives Club of the
Mid-Hudson Valley
Nelson House, Poughkeepsie

Rochester Sales Executives Club
Rochester Chamber of Commerce

Sales Executives Club of the
Mohawk Valley (Rome,
Utica)
Trinkhaus Manor, Rome

Sales Executives Club of Central New York
University Club, Syracuse

Sales Executives Club of Westchester
(White Plains)

NORTH CAROLINA

Western North Carolina Sales
Executives Club
Battery Park Hotel, Asheville

Charlotte Sales Executives Club
Hotel Charlotte

Durham Sales Executives Club
Hope Valley Country Club

Piedmont Sales Executives
Mayfair Cafeteria, Greensboro

Raleigh Sales Executives Club
Raleigh Country Club

Salisbury Sales Executives Club
Yadkin Hotel

Cape Fear Sales Executives
Club
Cape Fear Hotel (Wilmington)

Winston-Salem Sales Executives
Club
Old Town Club & Hotel Robert
E. Lee

NORTH DAKOTA

Fargo–Moorhead Sales Executives
P. O. Box 1271, Fargo

OHIO

Sales Executives Club of Akron
Akron City Club & Mayflower
Hotel

Canton Sales Executives Club
Belden & St. Francis Hotels

Cincinnati Sales Executives
Council
Netherland Plaza Hotel

Sales Executives Club of Cleveland
Hollenden Hotel

Columbus Sales Executives
Club
Fort Hayes Hotel

Sales Executives Club of East
Central Ohio (Coshocton)
Coshocton Country Club

Dayton Sales Executives Club
Biltmore Hotel

Sales Executives Club of North
Central Ohio (Mansfield)
Mansfield–Leland Hotel

Toledo Sales Executives Club
Toledo Club

Mahoning Valley Sales Executives Club (Youngstown)
Youngstown Country Club

OKLAHOMA
Oklahoma City Sales Executives
Club
Oklahoma Club

Tulsa Sales Executives Club
Hotel Tulsa

OREGON
Portland Sales Executives Club
Multnomah Hotel

PENNSYLVANIA
Allentown–Bethlehem Sales
Executives Club
Lehigh Valley Club (Allentown)

National Sales Executives of
Delaware County (Chester)

Springhaven Country Club
Easton Area Sales Executives
(Easton)
Hotel Easton

Sales Executives Club of Erie
Lawrence Hotel

Sales Executives Club of Greater
Harrisburg
Van's Colonial Restaurant

Sales Executives Club of Lan-
caster
Hotel Brunswick

Sales Managers' Association of
Philadelphia
Bellevue-Stratford Hotel

Sales Executives Club of Pittsburgh
Hotel William Penn

Sales Executives Club of Metro-
politan Reading
Berkshire Hotel

Sales Executives Club of Wilkes-
Barre–Scranton
Hotel Sterling (Wilkes-Barre)

Sales Executives Association of
York
Penn Hotel

RHODE ISLAND
Sales Managers' Club of Provi-
dence
Sheraton Biltmore Hotel

SOUTH CAROLINA
Columbia Sales Executives Club
Hotel Wade Hampton

Greenville Sales Executives
Club
Greenville Hotel

TENNESSEE
Chattanooga Sales Executives
Club
Pattern Hotel

Knoxville Sales Executives
Club
S and W Cafeteria

Memphis Sales Executives Club
University Club

Nashville Sales Executives
Council
Andrew Jackson Hotel

TEXAS

Abilene Sales Executives Club
Drake Hotel

Amarillo Sales Executives Club
Place varies

Sales Executives Club of Austin
Stephen F. Austin Hotel

Sabino Area Sales Executives
Club
Hotel Edison (Beaumont)

Corpus Christi Sales Executives
Club
Driscoll Hotel

Dallas Sales Executives Club,
Inc.
Melrose Hotel

El Paso Sales Executives Club
Paso del Norte Hotel

Fort Worth Sales Executives
Club
Hotel Texas

Houston Sales Executives Club
Ben Milam Hotel

San Antonio Sales Executives
Club
Plaza Hotel

East Texas Sales Executives
Club (Tyler, Jacksonville,
Longview)
Blackstone Hotel (Tyler)

UTAH

Utah Association of Sales Executives
Hotel Utah, Salt Lake City

VIRGINIA

Hampton Roads Sales Executives Club
Norfolk Yacht & Country Club

The Sales Executives Club of
Richmond, Inc.
Jefferson Hotel

Roanoke Sales Executives Club
Patrick Henry Hotel

WASHINGTON

Sales Executives Club of Seattle,
Inc.
Benjamin Franklin Hotel

Spokane Sales Executives Club
Desert Caravan Inn

Tacoma Sales Executives Club
University–Union Club

WEST VIRGINIA

Bluefield Sales Executives Club
Bluefield Country Club

The Sales Executives Club of
Huntington
Pritchard Hotel

Charleston Sales Executives
Council
Daniel Boone Hotel

WISCONSIN

National Sales Executives of
Madison
Hoffman House

Sales Executives Club of Milwaukee
Milwaukee Athletic Club

Sales Executives of Northeastern
Wisconsin (Neenah, Menasha,
Appleton, Oshkosh, Green
Bay)
North Shore Golf Club, Menasha

Sales Executive Council of
Racine
Manufacturers Association of
Racine

Index